LINDA FRASER'S
QUICK & EASY
SUPPERS

BBC BOOKS' QUICK AND EASY COOKERY SERIES

L aunched in 1989 by Ken Hom and Sarah Brown, the *Quick and Easy Cookery* series is a culinary winner. Everything about the titles is aimed at quick and easy recipes – the ingredients, the cooking methods and the menu section at the back of the books. Eight pages of colour photographs are also included to provide a flash of inspiration for the frantic or faint-hearted.

OTHER TITLES IN THE SERIES ALREADY PUBLISHED:

Beverley Piper's Quick & Easy Healthy Cookery
Clare Connery's Quick & Easy Salads
Joanna Farrow's Quick & Easy Fish Cookery
Ken Hom's Quick & Easy Chinese Cookery
Madhur Jaffrey's Quick & Easy Indian Cookery
Sandeep Chatterjee's Quick & Easy Indian Vegetarian Cookery
Sarah Brown's Quick & Easy Vegetarian Cookery
Shaun Hill's Quick & Easy Vegetable Cookery
Claire MacDonald's Quick & Easy Desserts and Puddings
Mary Berry's Quick & Easy Cakes

TO COME

Joanna Farrow's Quick & Easy Cake Decorating
Simone Sekers' Quick & Easy Preserves
Thane Prince's Quick & Easy Soups

LINDA FRASER'S
QUICK & EASY
SUPPERS

BBC BOOKS

To Allan, for all the good times

Published by BBC Books,
a division of BBC Enterprises Limited,
Woodlands, 80 Wood Lane
London W12 0TT

First published 1993
© Linda Fraser 1993
ISBN 0 563 36904 3

BBC Quick & Easy is a trademark of
the British Broadcasting Corporation

Designed by Peter Bridgewater
Illustrations by Lorraine Harrison
Photographs © James Murphy
Styling by Jane McLeish
Home Economist: Allyson Birch

Set in Bembo by Create Publishing Services Ltd, Bath

Printed and bound in Great Britain by Clays Ltd, St Ives Plc
Colour separation by Technik Ltd, Berkhamsted
Colour sections printed by Lawrence Allen Ltd, Weston-super-Mare
Cover printed by Clays Ltd, St Ives Plc

CONTENTS

INTRODUCTION

What is supper? When I was a child, it was a snack eaten just before bedtime. The evening meal, known as tea, was served at about 5 o'clock and included a main course, eaten with buttered bread, followed by a pudding and then, often as not, we had biscuits or cakes with a cup of tea to finish off!

Dinner, a main course and another pudding, was something we ate in the middle of the day. But nowadays the midday meal is more usually called lunch, and dinner has become a more special, two-, three- or even four-course evening meal, served later in the evening usually at the weekend and often including guests or friends.

So, what do we call the modern, mid-week evening meal which is (or should be) a smaller, healthier affair than either tea or dinner. It needs to be quick to cook and eat – just like the traditional bedtime snack – but be a more substantial, proper meal. Supper seems to me to be ideal   a simple, snappy name for a simple, snappy meal.

BE PREPARED

Today, everyone is so busy and, mid-week especially, we seem to have an ever-decreasing time to cook – and eat – so meals that have a minimum of preparation and cook either quickly or with little supervision have become an essential of modern life. It only takes a quick glance in a supermarket chiller cabinet to see the demand for fast food. Ready meals are taking over! But, do we have to buy these expensive ready-prepared dishes? Marketing consultants have apparently forecast that within a few years ready meals will have virtually replaced home-cooked food. Yet, as Derek Cooper commented in a recent article, 'A freshly cooked meal is different every time, whereas conveyor belt food never changes'. There are hundreds of dishes that can be put together in an amazingly short time, so let your store-cupboard be an inspiration – and keep on cooking!

To cook quickly, you do need to get a little bit organized – meals can't be made out of thin air. There are a number of basic store-cupboard necessities that you should stock up on, and a few simple, yet essential, pieces of good-quality cooking equipment that, to be honest, you can't really do without (see pages 11 and 12).

SHOPPING AROUND

Shopping can take an inordinate amount of time, so I've tried to keep the ingredients simple and easy to find. All of them can be found in large, city supermarkets, but in some areas you may have to seek out local specialist shops or a good delicatessen for good-quality, or more unusual, items. Do remember though that supermarkets only sell what there is a demand for, so pester your local supermarket manager if there is something that you feel he should stock.

One of the benefits of supermarkets is that many ingredients are, to varying degrees, pre-prepared. And when time is the critical factor foods that are ready to cook are a real bonus. You do, of course, have to pay for this extra preparation and its accompanying speed. Boneless, chicken breasts, for instance, are more expensive than those with a bone and if the skin is already removed they are more expensive still. Whole lettuces are a lot cheaper than bags of pre-prepared salads, but they take extra time and effort to wash.

In the end, you have to decide whether you have the time to save money – or whether a few well-prepared ingredients are worth the extra cost.

TAKING TIME OUT

At the beginning of each recipe, I have given the preparation and cooking time. To be consistent, I have worked out preparation time as the total time it takes to get the ingredients ready before cooking begins. However, do read the recipe through before you start, since quite often you may only need to prepare one or two ingredients before you start and then fit in preparing the others while the cooking is going on.

Don't be put off by the stated cooking time. In some recipes it is extremely short and the likelihood is that you will have to be around to stir, or turn – or simply get the plates ready! When the cooking time is longer, it may entail some hands-on cooking, but the time will also often include either in-the-oven or on-the-hob cooking that is essentially unsupervised, so you can get on with something else while you wait.

MAKING A MEAL OF IT

The recipes in this book are often a complete meal in themselves, but sometimes you will need to serve something else alongside – the choice will usually be determined by how hungry you are.

Take the cooking time into account. If a recipe cooks particularly quickly, you may have to start the accompaniment first. Perhaps putting cooking water on to boil, or preparing and chopping vegetables before you start.

BREAD

Bread is the fastest starchy accompaniment and good with almost everything.

PASTA

Even from frozen, fresh pasta can take less than 5 minutes to cook and most dried pasta takes only 10 or 12 minutes. Pasta is best with saucier main dishes.

LONG-GRAIN RICE

Also good with more moist foods, long-grain rice cooks in as little as 10 minutes.

POTATOES

These go with just about everything and take only 20 minutes to boil and are even faster cooked in the microwave.

BULGAR WHEAT

Bulgar wheat is great if you are short of space on the hob as it needs no cooking at all, just soak it in boiling water for 10–15 minutes.

FRESH VEGETABLES

Most are relatively quick to cook, but when you are in a hurry, choose really speedy ones like cabbage, broccoli, green beans, cauliflower or mangetout.

FROZEN AND CANNED VEGETABLES

Some frozen vegetables, such as peas and broad beans, and canned varieties, such as sweetcorn or beans, are ideal for fast meals.

SALADS

Salads are really quick, especially if you choose tight-leaved varieties of lettuce that need little washing, such as chicory, radicchio, fennel or iceberg lettuce. If you buy mixed bags of ready-prepared leaves, the salad will take only the time needed to mix up a dressing.

SAUCY ACCOMPANIMENTS

Chutneys and relishes, mustard and ready-prepared sauces (which includes everything from mayonnaise, through mint sauce to fresh tomato sauce) are good to serve with drier foods such as grilled meats and fish.

Ring the changes

Many people, myself included, never really follow a recipe – they use it instead as a guide to timing, simply as something to work from, or as inspiration to combine new ingredients. And while I'd like to suggest that everyone tries out these recipes at least once as they are (since I spent so much time getting them right!), they are essentially just suggestions.

If you are short of one – or even two or three – of the ingredients, then substitute others, or double up on one of the other ingredients. For instance, you might use a spice blend in place of individual spices; substitute fresh parsley for basil or use dried herbs in place of fresh (using half the quantity); add peas instead of sweetcorn or two red peppers instead of one green and one yellow.

When you use substitutes, there are a few basic rules to follow:

● Choose alternatives that cook in the same length of time (when you use different vegetables, meats or fish, for instance).

● Use ingredients that have much the same flavour and texture or consistency (such as soured cream in place of yoghurt or canned salmon instead of tuna) – unless, of course, you want to change the dish into something completely different!

● Keep the total quantity of the dish the same as, otherwise, you may affect the cooking time – and the number of people that the dish serves.

GETTING EQUIPPED

A well-equipped kitchen obviously makes quick cooking easier. You'll presumably already have several basic items, add others as you need them.

FOOD PROCESSOR

This is the only really expensive item I would recommend, though it isn't absolutely essential since, in effect, a food processor only speeds up laborious processes like chopping, puréeing and mixing. You can do without.

CHOPPING BOARDS

The modern polyboards are easy to clean, but I'd have to say I still return to my huge wooden board, which is big enough to work on without everything falling off the edges, yet still fits, end-on, into the sink, so I can give it a good scrub. Keep a second smaller board exclusively for chopping raw meat. And, if you have the space, a really little one for crushing garlic (I always crush garlic under the blade of a large knife, rather than using a garlic crusher, which, in my experience, always traps half of the garlic and is so difficult to clean).

KNIVES

Four knives are all you need, but they do have to be good quality – there are some excellent branded, stainless-steel knives on the market. Choose one large cook's chopping knife, one smaller general-purpose knife, one small serrated knife (for fruit and vegetables) and a decent bread knife. You'll also need a steel to keep the plain blades sharp.

COOKING PANS AND DISHES

One huge pan is essential for pasta. If you choose a good heavy-based one it will double as a jam pan or to use for stock or soups. And you'll find it also comes in handy for cooking big pots of chilli for a party, or for making two or three quantities of a recipe to freeze in batches.

You'll also need:

• two large pans for potatoes, vegetables and rice. If you are short on cupboard space, buy flameproof casseroles instead (see below).

• one medium pan for sauces – I prefer a non-stick pan for these, but you can't use metal utensils. If you like to whisk sauces, go for an enamelled cast-iron pan instead.

• one large, deep-sided frying-pan or sauté pan with a lid – this is my most used pan, I cook everything from stews through to stir-fries in it. The wide base means that you can fry foods like fish fillets, burgers and chicken breasts all in one batch.

• one smaller frying-pan with sloping sides for omelettes – non-stick pans are ideal.

• at least one large, lidded casserole. Choose one that is flameproof, so that it can double as a saucepan, if needed.

• several ovenproof baking dishes – for versatility, choose ones that are about 5 cm (2 in) deep.

ASSORTED BITS AND BOBS

• a colander and a big sieve.

• a vegetable peeler – I prefer those with a swivel action for speed and ease of use.

• a salad spinner – these are bulky, but I think essential for drying the leaves properly.

• several wooden spoons.

• a large slotted spoon.

• a balloon whisk – I also have a wonderful little whisk called a magic spoon, which makes amazingly quick work of whizzing together a salad dressing.

• a pair of good-quality kitchen scissors.

• a good stout pastry brush or paint-brush for basting with oil – avoid those with nylon bristles which melt on contact with hot food.

• a decent grater – I'd avoid the little rotary graters, which I find are a bit of a nuisance to clean, and go for a square-sided, free-standing grater with both large and small holes.

WHAT'S IN STORE?

Obviously the size of your kitchen cupboards, fridge and freezer will determine just how well stocked you can be. Don't just go out and buy everything on the lists, but build up your store gradually, making a note of things that you use a lot and of ingredients for recipes that you like (or would like) to cook.

The following lists include foods that I always have in my kitchen and they have all come in extremely handy – especially when I thought there was nothing in the house to eat!

IN THE GARDEN — OR ON A WINDOW-SILL

I only recently discovered how useful a garden can be as a store. I moved to a house with a garden – and my husband discovered that he likes to grow vegetables. We did have rather too many onions, leeks, beetroot, and salad burnet, which is a slightly obscure herb that he took a fancy to. But this year, I've steered him towards less quantity and more variety – with a selection of herbs, green vegetables, tomatoes and lettuces, which, along with the onions and leeks, will be more useful. There is a limit to what you can do with great quantities of beetroot and salad burnet.

Yet, even if you have no garden you can still grow all sorts of fresh herbs on a sunny window-sill – mint, rosemary, thyme, marjoram, basil, parsley and chives are all easy to grow and many supermarkets and greengrocers sell small tubs of growing herbs throughout the year. As a bonus, if you have a balcony or patio that gets some sun, one or two tomato plants, and even a lettuce or two, will grow quite happily throughout the summer.

IN THE KITCHEN

There are some foods that you should have in the house all the time. These are:
- a loaf of bread
- sea salt, either coarse in a grinder or fine in a tub

- peppercorns in a grinder
- a head of garlic
- potatoes
- onions
- one or two lemons

IN THE FRIDGE

This isn't a list of essentials, but they are useful to have at hand.
- a bottle or carton of milk
- a packet of unsalted butter
- small cartons of natural yoghurt and double cream
- a jar of mayonnaise
- cheese – Parmesan and a good-quality mature Cheddar are the best stand-bys
- fresh-cut herbs, if you have no plants – keep them in sealed polythene bags
- salad leaves – again, wash if necessary and store in sealed polythene bags
- tomatoes
- celery, carrots and spring onions

IN THE FREEZER

A well-stocked freezer is a boon, especially if you also have a microwave or, as I call it, a de-freezer (since this is by far its most useful attribute).
- one or two loaves of bread (remember that crusty loaves freeze least successfully)
- a packet of unsalted butter
- packets of shortcrust and puff pastry
- piece of fresh root ginger
- home-prepared fresh breadcrumbs (freeze these in a bag, so they stay loose, and use straight from the freezer)
- a small packet of leaf or chopped spinach
- small packets of peas and broad beans
- tubs of fresh tomato sauce (home-made if you've the time)
- fresh stock (again home-made if you've time)
- fresh pasta
- fish fillets
- minced lamb or beef
- grated Cheddar and Parmesan cheeses – pack loose into polythene bags to use straight from the freezer
- a piece of Stilton

• chopped herbs – chop fresh herbs and store in tubs or polythene bags, then spoon out the required amount and pop the rest straight back in the freezer – useful for stirring into cooked dishes

IN THE STORE-CUPBOARD

This list on first reading seems awfully long, but it is comprehensive. The dried items will keep almost indefinitely and things such as oils will keep in a cool dark cupboard for months on end.

DRIED GOODS

• several packets of dried pasta (include stuffed tortellini as well as plain varieties)
• a packet each of white and brown long-grain rice and a mix of rice and wild rice
• a packet of bulgar wheat
• a selection of dried herbs and spices (dried thyme and oregano, curry powder, cumin, coriander, turmeric, chilli powder and cinnamon are the most useful)
• packets of red, green and brown lentils
• good-quality stock cubes (in quick, cooked dishes, these make quite a creditable substitute for the real thing which, if you have it, can be kept in the freezer)

OILS AND VINEGARS

• a large bottle of olive oil – you'll notice as you try out the recipes (I hope) that I use olive oil almost all of the time. I know it is expensive, but it is healthier than other fats and oils. Go for extra virgin oil, which is the best, but if you find that the flavour is a little overpowering, then use half sunflower oil, or look out for one of the 'light' olive oils which aren't light on calories, but rather, light on flavour since they are a mixture of refined olive oil and extra virgin olive oil
• a large bottle of sunflower oil
• small bottles of walnut and sesame oils (for nutty flavoured salad dressings – expensive, but good to mix with olive or sunflower oils)
• small bottles of balsamic vinegar (again, this costs more than other vinegars, but it has a delightful, sweet aromatic flavour and once you have tasted it you will have difficulty buying anything else for salad dressings)
• bottles of white wine and sherry vinegars

SAUCES AND CONDIMENTS

- a small bottle of soy sauce
- a small bottle of Worcestershire sauce
- a jar of pesto
- tubes of tomato purée – or better still, look out for jars of sun-dried tomato paste which has a wonderful, sweet strong flavour (keep both in the fridge once opened)
- a jar of honey
- a jar of Dijon or wholegrain mustard (keep in the fridge once opened)
- jars of chutney, relishes and sauces (I have to include brown sauce and tomato ketchup) – again keep in the fridge once open
- a jar of sun-dried tomatoes in olive oil
- a jar of capers

SEEDS AND NUTS

- packets of almonds, hazelnuts and pine nuts (useful for scattering in salads)
- packets of sunflower, pumpkin and sesame seeds (again good for salads)

DRINKS

- a bottle or a box of dry white wine (use one that you would drink – the taste is important, even for cooking, and, after all, there is bound to be some left over from the recipe)
- a half bottle of sherry and a dry vermouth, such as Noilly Prat
- a carton of long-life milk (useful for the cornflakes, if nothing else)

CANS

- tuna fish in oil
- salmon – either pink or red
- anchovy fillets in oil
- cannellini, kidney, butter, flageolet and haricot beans (dare I add baked beans in tomato sauce?)
- chick peas
- sweetcorn kernels
- chopped tomatoes (look out for cans that include chopped herbs, or fennel and spices, which I particularly like)
- pimentos (peeled red peppers)

FISH AND SHELLFISH

It is a sad fact that we live on an island, surrounded by seas positively teeming with fish, yet we are not, on the whole, a nation of fish lovers. As Keith Floyd pointed out in one of his books, 'We must be the only country in the world that virtually needs an Act of Parliament passed to make us eat fish'! The fact, though, that many of us are eating less meat, means that we are beginning to look less warily at fish.

I love it. In fact, fish is definitely my favourite food. I'm lucky enough to have a really excellent fish shop nearby, and there is always a long queue, spilling out on to the pavement, on a Saturday. They aren't anything like as busy during the week and I'm sure the reason is that mid-week whole fish (what with all the scales, and heads and tails) becomes a bit of a fiddle. So, perhaps the fact that supermarkets now sell neat, plastic-cocooned, portions is a blessing in disguise.

The beauty of fish, I think, is its variety. When people announce that they don't like fish, I always want to ask, yes, but which one? They are all so different. I've stuck to easily available fish for the recipes in this chapter, using canned and smoked fish as well as fresh, which are pre-prepared where possible. And since I think that we should be encouraging our children to like fish too, many of the recipes are fairly simple fare. If your children are a bit wary, then start with recipes using flaked fish. I'm sure it won't be long before, like mine, they will be quite happy to tackle a whole trout.

SARDINE
AND TOMATO GALETTES

S E R V E S
—— 4 ——

PREPARATION TIME
20 minutes
COOKING TIME
15 minutes

225 g (8 oz) ready-made
puff pastry
A little flour for dusting
2 × 120-g (4.23-oz) cans
sardines in olive oil,
drained
225 g (8 oz) cherry
tomatoes, halved
2 tablespoons chopped fresh
basil plus extra shredded
basil to serve
Salt and freshly ground black
pepper
Soured cream to serve

If you haven't any puff pastry make a more rustic version using a stick of French bread instead – it needs to be about 30 cm (12 in) long. Cut in half lengthways then crossways and hollow out each piece slightly, brush with a little melted butter and bake in the oven for 10 minutes. Add the filling and bake for a further 5 minutes. Eat with a mixed leaf salad or some lightly fried courgettes.

Pre-heat the oven to gas mark 7, 220°C (425°F).

Cut the pastry into 4 and roll out each piece on a lightly floured board to a 13-cm (5-in) round. Damp the edges and fold over 1 cm (½ in) all around each, pressing the edge with a fork to stick it down. Prick the bases and place on a baking sheet and chill for 10 minutes, then bake the galettes for 10 minutes.

Meanwhile, break up the sardines with a fork. Remove the galettes from the oven and pile the sardines and tomatoes on top. Scatter the basil over the top and season to taste with salt and freshly ground black pepper. Bake for a further 5 minutes, then serve at once with a dollop of soured cream and a little more basil on each.

RED MULLET IN PARCELS WITH HERBS AND LEMON

SERVES

— 4 —

If you make the parcels from foil, you could cook them on the barbecue. Serve with boiled new potatoes and spinach cooked with a little cream and flavoured with freshly grated nutmeg, or a salad made with slightly bitter leaves, such as rocket, chicory, radicchio and frisée.

Pre-heat the oven to gas mark 6, 200°C (400°F). Cut four squares of foil or non-stick baking paper large enough to enclose each fish and brush with a little oil.

Wash the red mullet, remove the scales and then gut, or ask your fishmonger to do this for you which will reduce the preparation time. Pat the fish dry and tuck a herb sprig into each one. Place each fish on a piece of foil or paper, add a lemon wedge to each and season to taste with salt and freshly ground black pepper. Close the parcels, folding over the edges to seal, then place them in a baking tin and bake for about 15 minutes.

INGREDIENTS

PREPARATION TIME
15 minutes
COOKING TIME
15 minutes

2 tablespoons olive oil
4 red mullet, about
175–225 g (6–8 oz) each
4 sprigs of fresh basil, thyme
or rosemary
½ lemon, cut into four wedges
Salt and freshly ground black
pepper

SALMON FILLETS WITH TOMATO AND HERB SALSA

SERVES

—— 4 ——

PREPARATION TIME
5 minutes
COOKING TIME
15 minutes

25 g (1 oz) unsalted butter
1 tablespoon olive oil
4 salmon fillets, about 175 g
  (6 oz) each
Salt and freshly ground black
  pepper
FOR THE SALSA
2 tablespoons olive oil
1 tablespoon red wine
  vinegar
A few drops of hot pepper
  sauce or a pinch of chilli
  powder
2 tablespoons snipped fresh
  chives
2 tablespoons chopped fresh
  parsley
425-g (15-oz) can chopped
  tomatoes, drained

T his dish only takes about 20 minutes from start to finish, so if you want to have accompaniments, you may have to think about them before you begin. Fresh pasta and vegetables such as mangetout, French beans or courgettes can be cooked while the salmon is cooking. Don't overcook the salmon – it should flake easily, but be just done in the centre. If you prefer, you could heat up the salsa, rather than serving it cold.

Heat the butter and 1 tablespoon of the oil in a large frying-pan. Season the salmon fillets with salt and freshly ground black pepper and add to the pan. Cook over a medium heat for 4–5 minutes.

Meanwhile, mix together all the ingredients for the salsa, or whizz them together in a food processor if you prefer a smoother textured sauce.

Turn over the salmon fillets and cook for 4–5 minutes on the other side. Serve hot with a little of the pan juices spooned over. Serve the salsa on the side.

GRILLED SHELLFISH WITH PEPPERS AND TOMATOES WITH LEMON DRESSING

S E R V E S
—— 2 ——

This is really a summer-time dish, for eating on a Saturday evening, when you've had time to visit the fishmonger in the morning. Serve this dish with chunks of warm, crusty French bread to mop up the dressing. If you can't find raw prawns, use cooked ones and grill them for only a minute or two to heat through. Large prawns are wonderful, but eating them is a messy business. Provide big napkins and small bowls of warm water for each person.

Peel the skin from the peppers using a swivel action vegetable peeler. Lay the peppers, skinned side up in a roasting tin and brush with olive oil. Grill for 3–4 minutes. While they are cooking, score the squid with a very sharp knife in a fine criss-cross pattern and cut across into thick strips. Turn over the peppers, add the squid to the roasting tin, brush with olive oil and cook for 6 minutes.

Meanwhile, make the dressing: mix together the lemon juice and rind with the vinegar and oil and season to taste with salt and freshly ground black pepper. Mix in the chopped herbs.

Tuck the prawns in around the peppers, pour over the dressing and cook for 2 minutes. Add the tomatoes and scallops to the grill pan and cook for 8–10 minutes more turning the peppers, squid and prawns once or twice. Serve at once with the cooking juices poured over the top.

INGREDIENTS

PREPARATION TIME
5 minutes
COOKING TIME
22 minutes

½ *red and* ½ *yellow pepper, de-seeded and halved*
4 *small, prepared squid, halved lengthways*
8 *large raw prawns*
2 *plum or other firm tomatoes, quartered*
4 *large scallops*
FOR THE DRESSING
grated rind and juice of 1 lemon
2 *tablespoons white wine vinegar*
8 *tablespoons olive oil*
Salt and freshly ground black pepper
A few fronds of fresh fennel, chopped
2 *tablespoons chopped fresh parsley*

MONKFISH BROCHETTES WITH LEMON AND CHIVE SAUCE

SERVES

—— 4 ——

PREPARATION TIME
20 minutes
COOKING TIME
15 minutes

*450 g (1 lb) monkfish, cut
into 2.5-cm (1-in) chunks
1 orange and 1 yellow
pepper, de-seeded and cut
into 2.5-cm (1-in) squares
2 tablespoons extra virgin
olive oil
Salt and freshly ground black
pepper*
FOR THE SAUCE
*1 shallot, peeled and finely
chopped
4 tablespoons dry white wine
or white wine vinegar
Grated rind and juice of 1
lemon
150 g (5 oz) butter, diced
4 tablespoons snipped fresh
chives
Salt and freshly ground black
pepper*

The sauce is a *beurre blanc*, which sounds a bit posh for a supper book. It is, however, very easy to do and tastes really rather wonderful. It has to be made at the last minute though, since it doesn't like to be kept warm. Use thick fillets of cod or haddock, if you prefer, and remember, if you use wooden skewers soak them in warm water first to help prevent them burning. Serve the brochettes with deep-fried celeriac or potato chips and some mangetout and baby sweetcorn.

———

Thread the monkfish and peppers alternately onto wooden skewers. Brush with olive oil and season to taste with salt and freshly ground black pepper. Grill for 5–8 minutes, brushing them occasionally with oil until the fish is cooked and turning golden brown.

Meanwhile, make the sauce. Place the shallot in a small pan, pour in the wine or vinegar and the lemon rind and juice. Bring to the boil and allow to bubble up until the liquid has reduced by half the original quantity. Turn down the heat until it is very low and add the butter, piece by piece, whisking continuously until you have a nice creamy sauce. Stir in the chives and season to taste with salt and freshly ground black pepper. Serve at once with the brochettes.

Baked mackerel with mustard and orange butter

SERVES
— 4 —

Mackerel were always difficult fish, often too big to serve whole and full of little bones, but far too much of a fiddle to fillet, especially yourself. Now you can buy fillets from the supermarket which are a much better size – and they've no bones. The sauce also goes well with trout.

Pre-heat the oven to gas mark 4, 180°C (350°F).

Lay the mackerel fillets, skin-side down in a shallow buttered baking dish. Pour over the orange juice, add salt and freshly ground black pepper to taste and bake, uncovered, for 10 minutes.

Place the garlic, mustard and orange rind in a small bowl and beat in the butter. Dot over the mackerel and bake for 5 minutes more until the mackerel is cooked.

INGREDIENTS

PREPARATION TIME
10 minutes
COOKING TIME
15 minutes

4 large mackerel fillets
Grated rind and juice of 1 orange
Salt and freshly ground black pepper
1 garlic clove, peeled and crushed
2 teaspoons wholegrain mustard
25 g (1 oz) butter, softened

SPICED TROUT WITH ALMONDS

S E R V E S

—— 4 ——

PREPARATION TIME
5 minutes
COOKING TIME
15 minutes

1 tablespoon plain flour
½ teaspoon ground cardamom
½ teaspoon ground coriander
½ teaspoon turmeric
1 teaspoon ground cumin
4 trout, about 175 g (6 oz)
 each
Salt and freshly ground black
 pepper
50 g (2 oz) butter
2 tablespoons olive oil
50 g (2 oz) flaked almonds
150 ml (5 fl oz) double
 cream

T rout with almonds is a classic. Here I've added a blend of aromatic spices to the recipe, which makes it particularly delicious. Serve the trout without the cream, if you like, just pour over the pan juices instead.

Mix together the flour and spices in a polythene bag, pop in the trout and shake until the trout are coated. Season with salt and freshly ground black pepper.

Heat the butter and oil in a large frying-pan until foaming, then add the trout and fry over a medium heat for 8–10 minutes until the trout is cooked and the skin crisp and golden, turning once.

Add the almonds for the last minute or two and fry until golden. Lift the trout and almonds out of the pan with a slotted spoon and keep warm. Stir the cream into the pan juices, heat through on a very low heat, stirring all the time, add seasoning to taste and pour over the trout. Scatter the almonds on top and serve at once.

SAUCY POTATO-TOPPED FISH PIE

S E R V E S
—— 4 ——

My mother often made this pie when I was a child, her mother made it too – and now I'm making it for my children. Make it up the day before, if you like, then just bake when you are ready. Peas, or broad beans can replace the sweetcorn and you can posh it up a bit by adding a handful of cooked, peeled prawns or arranging sliced tomatoes on top of the sauce before you spoon on the potatoes. Use cod in place of haddock if you prefer.

Pre-heat the oven to gas mark 5, 190°C (375°F).

Boil the potatoes in salted water for 15–20 minutes until tender, then drain. Meanwhile, cook the eggs in boiling salted water for 7 minutes, then drain and cool under cold running water. Place the fish in a shallow pan and pour over all but 2 tablespoons of the milk. Cook the fish gently for 5–8 minutes. Lift it out of the pan and reserve the milk, then remove the skin and bones from the fish and break the flesh into large flakes.

Melt 25 g (1 oz) of the butter in a saucepan, stir in the flour and cook over a low heat for 1 minute. Remove the pan from the heat and gradually stir in the reserved milk. Return the pan to the heat and stir until boiling, thickened and smooth.

Shell the eggs and chop them roughly, stir into the sauce with the fish and sweetcorn and seasoning. Spoon into a lightly greased ovenproof dish. Mash the potatoes with the parsley, the 2 tablespoons of milk and the remaining butter, then add seasoning to taste and spoon over the fish mixture. Spread evenly and mark the top with a fork. Scatter over the cheese and bake for 30–35 minutes until the potato top is golden and the sauce bubbling. Serve at once.

INGREDIENTS

PREPARATION TIME
15 minutes
COOKING TIME
1 hour

550 g (1 ¼ lb) potatoes, peeled and cut into large chunks
2 eggs
225 g (8 oz) haddock fillets
225 g (8 oz) smoked haddock fillets
375 ml (13 fl oz) milk
50 g (2 oz) butter
25 g (1 oz) plain flour
200-g (7-oz) can sweetcorn, drained
Salt and freshly ground black pepper
3 tablespoons chopped fresh parsley
100 g (4 oz) mature Cheddar cheese, grated

GRILLED HERRING WITH APPLE AND BEETROOT

SERVES
—— 4 ——

Nowadays filleted herring is easy to find and just about solves the problem of the bones. Choose lightly pickled beetroot rather than fresh; either the kind that comes in jars, or the freshly cooked ones sold in the fruit and veg department in the supermarket. They give a lovely piquant flavour to the dish.

Brush the herrings with a little of the oil and season with salt and freshly ground black pepper. Grill for 5 minutes on each side.

Meanwhile, heat the remaining oil in a frying-pan, add the onion and fry over a medium heat for 5–8 minutes until soft and golden brown. Add the beetroot and apples and fry, stirring, for a minute or two to soften the apple. When the fish is ready, stir the mustard and cream into the apple mixture and add seasoning to taste. Spoon the apple mixture over the herrings, scatter with parsley and serve at once.

INGREDIENTS

PREPARATION TIME
10 minutes
COOKING TIME
10 minutes

4 filleted herrings, about
  125 g (5 oz) each
3 tablespoons olive oil
Salt and freshly ground black
  pepper
1 small onion, peeled and
  very finely chopped
100 g (4 oz) pickled
  beetroot, diced
2 dessert apples, peeled,
  cored and diced
¼ teaspoon wholegrain
  mustard
2 tablespoons double cream
2 tablespoons chopped fresh
  parsley

COD WITH BACON AND RED PEPPERS

SERVES

—— 4 ——

You can buy bacon chops vacuum-packed – ideal to pop in the freezer for emergencies. You could, of course, use ordinary bacon but add it once the cod is cooking, otherwise it will overcook in the time. Choose smoked rather than green or unsmoked bacon, as the flavour goes particularly well with the cod.

Heat the oil in a large frying-pan and add the peppers and bacon. Fry for 4–5 minutes until the peppers are softened and the bacon golden. Then add the cod fillets, season to taste with salt and freshly ground black pepper and cook over a medium heat for 5–6 minutes until the fillets are lightly browned underneath.

Turn them over and cook for 5–6 minutes more until the fish is cooked through. Serve at once.

INGREDIENTS

PREPARATION TIME
5 minutes
COOKING TIME
15 minutes

4 tablespoons olive oil
2 red peppers, de-seeded and cut into thin strips
2 smoked bacon chops, about 100 g (4 oz) each, cut into thin strips
4 thick cod tail fillets, about 100 g (4 oz) each
Salt and freshly ground black pepper

FISH AND PRAWN CURRY

SERVES
—— 4 ——

PREPARATION TIME
10 minutes
COOKING TIME
30 minutes

3 tablespoons sunflower oil
450 g (1 lb) monkfish, cod
    or haddock fillets, skinned
    if necessary and cut into
    chunks
175 g (6 oz) large cooked
    prawns, peeled
1 onion, peeled and finely
    chopped
1 garlic clove, peeled and
    crushed
2.5-cm (1-in) piece fresh
    root ginger, peeled and
    finely grated
2 dried red chillies, crushed
    or ½–1 teaspoon chilli
    powder
2 teaspoons ground cumin
2 teaspoons ground turmeric
225-g (8-oz) can chopped
    tomatoes
100 g (4 oz) creamed
    coconut, dissolved in
    300 ml (10 fl oz) boiling
    water
Juice of 1 lime or ½ lemon
Salt

You could make this dish with curry powder in place of the individual spices – choose a mild or medium hot one for this recipe. Monkfish, because it is so firm, is probably the best fish to use; with cod or haddock keep the pieces quite large otherwise they will break up a little during cooking. Serve with boiled long-grain and wild rice and lightly cooked mangetout or green beans.

Heat 2 tablespoons of the oil in a large, heavy-based pan and fry the fish for 2–3 minutes until lightly coloured. Add the prawns and cook for 1–2 minutes, then tip the contents of the pan out into a dish and keep warm. Heat the remaining oil in the pan and add the onion, garlic, ginger, chillies or chilli powder, cumin and turmeric and fry over a medium heat for 5–8 minutes until the onion is soft, stirring occasionally.

Add the tomatoes to the pan, then stir in the coconut liquid, lime or lemon juice and salt to taste. Bring to the boil and simmer, uncovered, for 10 minutes. Return the fish and prawns to the sauce and cook very gently for about 5 minutes until the fish is hot and cooked.

CREOLE SALMON

SERVES
— 4 —

Creole cooking is tasty and spicy. Here a dark spice mixture is used to coat salmon. Cod or haddock fillets can be used instead – thawed, frozen fillets or steaks are just fine. Or you could cut monkfish into chunks, coat them in the spice mixture, then thread onto skewers, drizzle with oil and cook under the grill or on a barbecue. A leafy green salad and new potatoes go very well with this.

Mix together the herbs, spices, garlic, salt and freshly ground pepper and rub over both sides of the salmon fillets.

Heat the butter and oil in a large frying-pan until foaming, then add the salmon fillets and cook for about 10 minutes until just cooked, turning them once. Spoon the pan juices over the salmon as you serve.

INGREDIENTS

PREPARATION TIME
5 minutes
COOKING TIME
10 minutes

1 teaspoon dried thyme or
    oregano
¼ teaspoon cayenne pepper
2 teaspoons paprika
1 garlic clove, peeled and
    crushed
1 teaspoon salt
1 teaspoon freshly ground
    black pepper
4 skinless salmon fillets,
    about 175 g (6 oz) each
25 g (1 oz) butter
2 tablespoons olive oil

FILLETS OF TROUT IN A HERB AND WINE SAUCE

SERVES

—— 4 ——

This is a very summery dish, but since all the ingredients are readily available all year round, there's no reason why you shouldn't make it to cheer up a chilly winter's day. Use salmon fillets or steaks if you like, they will take a few minutes more to cook on each side, but otherwise just follow the recipe as it is.

Melt the butter in a large frying-pan, add the trout fillets, skin-side up, and cook for 3 minutes until lightly browned. Turn them over carefully, scatter the cucumber over the top and cover the pan; cook for 3 minutes more.

Meanwhile, put the shallot or onion, wine, lemon juice and parsley stalks in a pan and boil hard until reduced by half. Remove the parsley stalks from the wine mixture and stir in the chopped parsley and mint and the double cream. Season to taste with cayenne pepper, salt and freshly ground black pepper, then pour over the trout and heat through for a minute or two before serving.

INGREDIENTS

PREPARATION TIME
10 minutes
COOKING TIME
15 minutes

25 g (1 oz) butter
4 trout fillets
½ cucumber, peeled, then halved lengthways, de-seeded and diced
1 shallot or ½ small onion, peeled and very finely chopped
150 ml (5 fl oz) white wine
Juice of ½ lemon
2–3 sprigs fresh parsley, chopped and stalks reserved
1 tablespoon chopped fresh mint
4 tablespoons double cream
Pinch of cayenne pepper
Salt and freshly ground black pepper

POTATO SALAD WITH TUNA AND ANCHOVIES

SERVES

—— 4 ——

The first tiny outdoor Jersey Royals that arrive in June will make this into a particularly fine salad. If the potatoes are really fresh and earthy, add some chopped fresh mint to the dressing along with the parsley, which will really bring out their flavour.

Cook the potatoes in boiling salted water for 15–20 minutes until just tender. Meanwhile, flake the tuna and place in a large bowl. Add the anchovies, shallot or onion and the olives. Make the dressing, by mixing together the oil, vinegar, garlic and parsley. Season to taste with salt and freshly ground black pepper and set aside.

As soon as the potatoes are tender, drain them and tip them into the bowl with the other ingredients. Pour over the dressing and toss together. Arrange the tomato slices on individual plates and spoon the potato salad on top, then serve while still warm with crusty bread to mop up the dressing.

INGREDIENTS

PREPARATION TIME
15 minutes
COOKING TIME
25 minutes

900 g (2 lb) small new
   potatoes, scrubbed
200-g (7-oz) can tuna fish
   in oil, drained
50-g (2-oz) can anchovy
   fillets, drained and
   chopped
1 shallot or ½ small onion,
   peeled and finely chopped
8 stoned black olives, cut
   into quarters
2 beefsteak tomatoes, sliced

FOR THE DRESSING
4 tablespoons olive oil
3 tablespoons balsamic or 2
   tablespoons white wine
   vinegar
2 garlic cloves, peeled and
   crushed
A large bunch of fresh
   parsley, finely chopped
Salt and freshly ground black
   pepper

FISH CAKES

S E R V E S

—— 4 ——

INGREDIENTS

PREPARATION TIME
15 minutes
COOKING TIME
30 minutes

*350 g (12 oz) potatoes,
  peeled and cut into chunks*
25 g (1 oz) butter
*1–2 tablespoons single cream
  or milk*
*350 g (12 oz) cooked,
  smoked or canned fish*
*2 tablespoons chopped fresh
  parsley*
*Salt and freshly ground black
  pepper*
*75 g (3 oz) fresh
  breadcrumbs*
1 egg, beaten
4 tablespoons sunflower oil

Make them with some good-quality canned red salmon if you are really rushed or, if you have a little more time, lightly cook some smoked haddock while the potatoes are cooking. If you use left-over potatoes, make sure they are floury ones – waxy ones don't mash at all well. Serve with a dollop of tartare sauce which you can make while the fish cakes are frying. Just stir 1 teaspoon each of snipped fresh chives and finely chopped parsley, capers and gherkins into 200 ml (7 fl oz) of mayonnaise.

Boil the potatoes in salted water for 15–20 minutes until tender, then drain and mash with the butter and cream or milk. Leave to cool completely, then add the flaked fish and mix into the potato with the parsley and salt and freshly ground black pepper to taste. Form the mixture into 8 flat rounds.

Spread out the breadcrumbs on one plate and the egg on another. Dip the cakes first in egg, then in breadcrumbs to coat completely. Heat the oil in large frying-pan and fry the fish cakes for about 8 minutes until golden brown and crisp on the outside, turning them once.

Opposite: GRILLED SHELLFISH WITH PEPPERS AND TOMATOES
WITH LEMON DRESSING (*page 21*)

POULTRY

When chickens, turkey and ducks were only sold whole, they were most often weekend or a festive fare, usually roasted whole. If you wanted portions, either you had to do this yourself or find a friendly butcher to do it for you. Nowadays, though, supermarket and butchers' shelves are positively teeming with portions, fillets, steaks, chunks, strips and even mince.

I've included two recipes for duck breasts, which I am rather partial to, but since the breasts are expensive – and the recipes particularly delicious – keep them for special suppers. Most of the other recipes are for chicken, but turkey pieces of the same size can be used instead – and vice versa for the turkey recipes. If you can, do buy free-range, corn-fed chicken, which is available in most supermarkets, because although it costs more, it tastes so much better.

Really good turkey is more difficult to find – the standard bird is seriously lacking in flavour. Farm-bred birds are generally better. Look for the Traditional Farm Fresh label which is a sign of quality.

Last year, I travelled out to the wilds of Essex to meet Derek Kelly who rears a completely different turkey, with bronze feathers instead of white – the plucked birds have what he likes to call designer stubble since the feather stubs are dark. These birds, strange to say, are bred for flavour (rather than size). He sells portions and mince from the farm, if you live close enough, otherwise, try your best local butcher – you may soon even find portions from bronze turkeys in your super-market. Look out for them because, in my opinion, turkey never tasted so good!

Opposite: WARM DUCK SALAD WITH CAPER AND HERB DRESSING (*page 36*)

WARM DUCK SALAD WITH CAPER AND HERB DRESSING

SERVES

—— 4 ——

T his is really a dish for posh suppers – reserve it for those occasions when you have something to celebrate. Duck breasts are not cheap and so you could easily substitute chicken breasts if you prefer. Alternatively, since this recipe is so delicious with the duck, you could use only two duck breasts and serve it as a starter for four people!

Heat 2 tablespoons of the oil in a large frying-pan, add the duck breasts and cook over a medium to high heat for 5–8 minutes until browned all over, yet still pink inside.

Meanwhile, make the dressing. Mix together the remaining oil with the vinegar and plenty of salt and freshly ground black pepper. Arrange the rocket or spinach on plates.

When the duck is cooked, lift it out of the pan with a slotted spoon. Pour the dressing into the pan, add the capers and herbs and simmer gently while you slice the duck breasts thickly. Arrange the duck breasts on top of the rocket or spinach and pour over the warm dressing. Serve at once.

INGREDIENTS

PREPARATION TIME
5 minutes
COOKING TIME
10 minutes

7 tablespoons extra virgin olive oil
4 duck breasts, skinned
3 tablespoons balsamic or white wine vinegar
Salt and freshly ground black pepper
150 g (5 oz) rocket or baby spinach leaves
3 tablespoons capers
4 tablespoons chopped mixed fresh herbs, such as parsley, chives, chervil and thyme

Turkey, Mushrooms and Broccoli in Filo Purses

SERVES

— 4 —

Filo pastry is available fresh as well as frozen in super-markets and Greek delicatessens. You need sixteen 18–20-cm (7–8-in) squares for this recipe. Some of the shop-bought sheets will be big enough to cut in two, others will only make one square each, in which case you will need sixteen sheets instead of eight. Eat with a tomato salad, or in a separate dish, bake some halved and seasoned tomatoes for 10–15 minutes at the same time as the purses.

Heat the oil in a large pan, add the turkey and garlic and fry for 5 minutes until browned, stirring frequently to break up the lumps. Add the mushrooms and broccoli and fry for 3–5 minutes more, then stir in the flour and cook for 1 minute. Pour in the milk and cook, stirring, until boiling and thickened. Stir in the olives and season to taste with salt and freshly ground black pepper, then tip out into a bowl and leave for about half an hour until cold, stirring occasionally.

Pre-heat the oven to gas mark 5, 190°C (375°F). Cut the filo pastry into sixteen 18–20-cm (7–8-in) squares and brush the top of each with a little olive oil.

Lay out 8 of the pastry squares on a floured surface. Next, place the other 8 pastry squares on top of the first 8, but at right angles so that each pair of pastry squares forms a Star of David shape where all the corners can be seen. Divide the turkey mixture among the 8 sets of pastry drawing up the corners to form 8 little round purses. Push the pastry together at the top of each to seal, then fluff out the corners. Place the purses on a baking sheet and brush with a little more oil. Bake for 15–20 minutes until the pastry is golden brown and the filling hot. Serve at once.

INGREDIENTS

PREPARATION TIME
40 minutes
COOKING TIME
45 minutes

4 tablespoons olive oil
225 g (8 oz) minced turkey
1 garlic clove, peeled and
  crushed
100 g (4 oz) button
  mushrooms
175 g (6 oz) broccoli, cut
  into tiny florets
1 tablespoon plain flour
150 ml (5 fl oz) milk
5 stoned black olives,
  chopped
Salt and freshly ground black
  pepper
16 18–20-cm (7–8-in)
  squares of filo pastry

BAKED CHICKEN BREASTS WITH PESTO

SERVES

—— 4 ——

This is one of those oh-so-simple recipes that tastes absolutely delicious. You need good chicken – corn-fed and free range. For the pesto you really must have extra virgin olive oil and fresh basil. Three handfuls makes a wonderfully flavoursome sauce, but you can cut the basil to just one handful if you are short – or add some parsley. It makes a slightly less intense, yet excellent, pesto. Use 4 tablespoons of shop-bought pesto if you haven't time to make your own. Serve with buttered noodles and a salad.

INGREDIENTS

PREPARATION TIME
5 minutes
COOKING TIME
30–35 minutes

4 boneless chicken breasts, skinned
3 handfuls basil leaves
1 garlic clove, peeled and crushed
4 tablespoons extra virgin olive oil
Salt
50 g (2 oz) Parmesan cheese, grated
2 tablespoons pine kernels

Pre-heat the oven to gas mark 4, 180°C (350°F).

Slash the chicken breasts 3 or 4 times, then arrange in a lightly greased shallow baking dish.

Place the basil leaves, garlic and olive oil in a food processor with a little salt and whizz until blended and smooth. Stop 2 or 3 times and scrape the mixture from the sides, down towards the bottom of the bowl, with a rubber spatula. Transfer to a bowl and stir in half of the cheese. Spread over the chicken pieces, working it into the slashes, then cover the dish and bake for 20 minutes.

Then raise the oven temperature to gas mark 6, 200°C (400°F), remove the lid, spoon over the juices, scatter the pine kernels and the remaining cheese over the top and bake for 10–15 minutes more until the chicken is cooked through and lightly browned. Serve at once.

STIR-FRIED CHICKEN AND VEGETABLES

SERVES

—— 4 ——

The secret of cooking stir-fries is to have a large pan. A wok is of course ideal, some would say essential, but it is possible to stir-fry in a frying-pan, so long as it is very large and you get it very hot before you add the oil. I often add a handful or two of cashew nuts and some sliced canned water chestnuts just because I like the added crunch.

Mix together the marinade ingredients, then add the chicken. Mix thoroughly and leave to stand for 5 minutes.

Heat a large frying-pan or wok, then add the sunflower or groundnut oil. Add the garlic and ginger and stir-fry for 10 seconds, then tip in the chicken mixture and stir-fry over a high heat for 2 minutes. Add the peppers and green beans and stir-fry for 2 minutes more.

Finally add the sherry, soy sauce and salt to taste. Serve at once with rice and a leafy salad.

INGREDIENTS

PREPARATION TIME
15 minutes
COOKING TIME
6 minutes

450 g (1 lb) boneless chicken breasts, skinned and cut into thin strips
1 tablespoon sunflower or groundnut oil
1 garlic clove, peeled and crushed
2.5-cm (1-in) piece fresh root ginger, peeled and grated
1 red and 1 yellow pepper, de-seeded and sliced
100 g (1 oz) thin French beans, halved
2 tablespoons dry sherry
1 tablespoon light soy sauce
Salt

FOR THE MARINADE
1 tablespoon light soy sauce
1 tablespoon dry sherry
2 teaspoons sesame oil
2 teaspoons cornflour

TURKEY BREAST STEAKS WITH MUSHROOMS

SERVES

—— 4 ——

Turkey breast steaks are quite small, so you might like to add one extra for anyone with a big appetite. Use chicken breasts or thighs instead if you prefer. As for the mushrooms, a mix of chestnut, shiitake and open-cup mushrooms is very good instead of plain button mushrooms.

Heat the oil in a large shallow pan, add the turkey breasts and fry for 3–4 minutes, then remove them from the pan and set aside. Add the onion and garlic to the pan and cook for 5 minutes, stirring occasionally, until softened. Add the mushrooms and cook for 2 minutes, then stir in the flour and cook for 1 minute more. Stir in the stock and bring to the boil, stirring all the time. Season to taste with salt and freshly ground black pepper, then return the turkey steaks to the pan, cover and simmer for 10–15 minutes until the turkey is tender. Stir in the parsley and serve hot.

INGREDIENTS

PREPARATION TIME
8 minutes
COOKING TIME
25 minutes

2 tablespoons olive oil
4 turkey breast steaks, about
    100 g (4 oz) each
1 small onion, peeled and
    finely chopped
1 garlic clove, peeled and
    crushed
350 g (12 oz) mixed
    mushrooms, sliced
1 tablespoon plain flour
300 ml (10 fl oz) chicken
    stock
Salt and freshly ground black
    pepper
2 tablespoons chopped fresh
    parsley

ONE-POT CHICKEN AND SPRING VEGETABLES

S E R V E S
— 4 —

C hicken thighs have a lovely meaty taste, but chicken drumsticks or breasts, or turkey steaks could be used here instead. If it isn't spring-time, then use ordinary turnip or swede and carrots and cut them into chunks. I have a very large deep sauté pan which I use for recipes like this, with plenty of room to fry the chicken in one batch. The wide surface area means that everything sits in the sauce and cooks evenly. Otherwise, use a flameproof casserole — if the base isn't large enough to fit the chicken in one layer, do the initial browning in two batches.

Heat the oil in a large sauté pan and fry the chicken pieces for about 5 minutes until golden brown all over. Lift them out of the pan with a slotted spoon and set aside. Reduce the heat slightly, then add the onion and garlic to the pan and fry over a medium heat for 5 minutes. Stir in the celery and cook for 3 minutes more. Add the vegetables and fry for 3–5 minutes until they are beginning to brown. Dust in the flour and cook for 1 minute, then gradually stir in the stock and cook until boiling and thickened.

Return the chicken to the pan, add seasoning to taste and cover the pan. Simmer for about 20 minutes until the chicken and vegetables are tender. Scatter the parsley over the top and serve.

INGREDIENTS

PREPARATION TIME
10 minutes
COOKING TIME
40 minutes

2 tablespoons olive oil
8 chicken thighs, skinned
1 large onion, peeled and
  finely sliced
2 garlic cloves, peeled and
  crushed
4 green celery sticks, sliced
8 baby turnips, scrubbed
8 baby carrots, scrubbed
8 baby sweetcorn
25 g (1 oz) plain flour
600 ml (1 pint) hot chicken
  stock
Salt and freshly ground black
  pepper
4 tablespoons chopped fresh
  parsley

SKEWERED TURKEY WITH A SPICY SAUCE

SERVES

—— 4 ——

PREPARATION TIME
32 minutes
COOKING TIME
15 minutes

1 garlic clove, peeled and
crushed
1 small onion, peeled and
very finely chopped
A dash of hot pepper sauce
Grated rind and juice of 1
orange
2 tablespoons soy sauce
1 tablespoon clear honey
2 teaspoons sesame, chilli or
stir-fry oil
Freshly ground black pepper
550 g (1 ¼ lb) turkey breast
meat or turkey steaks, cut
into 2.5-cm (1-in) cubes
2 tablespoons sesame seeds

These kebabs are especially good if you have the time to prepare them early in the day, or even the night before to let the turkey absorb the flavours from the marinade. Use a flavoured oil if you have some, otherwise olive or sunflower will do. Serve the kebabs with a mixed leaf salad and rice.

In a large bowl or plastic tub, mix together the garlic, onion, hot pepper sauce, orange rind and juice, soy sauce, honey, oil and pepper to make a marinade. Tip in the turkey cubes and stir to coat evenly. Leave to marinate for up to 30 minutes at room temperature, or place in the fridge until needed.

When you are ready to cook the turkey, lift the pieces out of the marinade and thread them onto skewers. Grill for 10 minutes, turning the skewers once or twice, then scatter the sesame seeds over the meat and grill for 3–5 minutes more until the turkey is browned and cooked through, but still moist.

Meanwhile, pour the marinade into a small pan and bring to the boil. Simmer for 3–5 minues until reduced slightly. Drizzle the sauce over the kebabs and serve.

RAGOUT OF CHICKEN WITH CARROTS AND HERBS

S E R V E S
—— 4 ——

The carrots give a delightful sweet touch to this ragout, don't cut the strips of carrot too thinly or they may break up as they cook. For a dinner party, you can create a slightly posher version: use tarragon in place of the thyme in the sauce, add 2 or 3 tablespoons of dry vermouth instead of some of the stock, then stir in a couple of tablespoonfuls of cream at the end.

———

Heat the oil in a large sauté pan and fry the chicken thighs until golden brown on all sides. Remove from the pan with a slotted spoon and set aside. Add the onion and garlic to the pan and fry over a medium heat for 5–8 minutes until softened and just beginning to brown. Stir in the flour and cook for 1 minute, then add the stock and bring to the boil, stirring all the time.

Return the chicken to the pan, add the herb sprigs and bay leaf and season to taste with salt and freshly ground black pepper. Cover and simmer for 25 minutes. Stir in the carrots and cook for 5–10 minutes more until the chicken is cooked and the carrots tender. Remove the bay leaf and herb sprigs, scatter over the chopped herbs and serve hot.

INGREDIENTS

PREPARATION TIME
15 minutes
COOKING TIME
1 hour

2 tablespoons olive oil
8 chicken thighs, skinned
1 onion, peeled and finely
  chopped
1 garlic clove, peeled and
  crushed
2 tablespoons plain flour
600 ml (1 pint) hot chicken
  stock
Few sprigs of thyme and
  parsley
1 bay leaf
Salt and freshly ground black
  pepper
350 g (12 oz) carrots, cut
  into matchsticks
1 tablespoon each chopped
  fresh parsley and thyme,
  and snipped fresh chives

CHICKEN TAGINE WITH TOMATOES

SERVES

—— 4 ——

INGREDIENTS

PREPARATION TIME
10 minutes
COOKING TIME
45 minutes

2 tablespoons olive oil
8 chicken thighs, skinned
1 onion, peeled and finely
  sliced
Pinch of saffron threads
900 g (2 lb) tomatoes,
  peeled and chopped
2.5-cm (1-in) piece fresh
  root ginger, peeled and
  finely grated
2 teaspoons ground cinnamon
Salt and freshly ground black
  pepper
2 tablespoons clear honey

A tagine is a North African – usually Moroccan – stew, it is named after the traditional cooking dish. The flavours are always sweet and sour – tagines often include fruits such as apricots, apples or prunes, but this one gains its sweetness from the tomatoes. The blend of fragrant spices is delicious with the chicken, use ½ teaspoon of ground ginger if you have no fresh. Serve the tagine with steamed bulgar wheat or couscous.

———

Heat the oil in a large, shallow pan, add the chicken thighs and onion and cook over a medium heat for 10 minutes, turning the chicken thighs over occasionally.

Meanwhile, soak the saffron threads in 2 tablespoons of boiling water for 5 minutes. Tip the saffron and its liquid into the chicken pan and add the tomatoes, ginger, cinnamon and seasoning to taste. Cover the pan and cook over a gentle heat for 15–20 minutes until the chicken is tender. Remove the chicken from the pan and keep warm. Stir the honey into the sauce and allow it to bubble up for a minute or two until it is reduced and thick. Return the chicken to the sauce, turn the thighs until thoroughly coated, then serve hot.

PAN-FRIED CHICKEN
WITH HERBS AND CREAM

S E R V E S
—— 4 ——

I f you have a bit more time leave the chicken breasts whole, rather than shredding them, and cook them over a low heat in the oil and butter for 10–12 minutes until cooked through. Buy corn-fed free range chicken if you can, it is a little more expensive than standard chicken, but in this simple recipe, you will really appreciate the difference in flavour. Serve the chicken with buttered spinach tagliatelle.

Heat the butter and oil in a frying-pan, add the chicken strips and cook over a fairly high heat for 5–6 minutes until golden brown. Add the garlic and courgettes and cook for 2–3 minutes, then pour over the vermouth or wine. Allow it to bubble up, then reduce the heat and add the herbs and salt and freshly ground black pepper to taste. Stir in the cream and cook for 1 minute. Serve at once.

INGREDIENTS

PREPARATION TIME
15 minutes
COOKING TIME
10 minutes

25 g (1 oz) butter
1 tablespoon olive oil
4 boneless chicken breasts, skinned and cut diagonally into thick strips
1 garlic clove, peeled and crushed
2 courgettes, sliced diagonally
2 tablespoons dry vermouth or dry white wine
2 tablespoons each chopped fresh parsley, oregano and thyme
2 tablespoons snipped fresh chives
Salt and freshly ground black pepper
150 ml (5 fl oz) double cream

*P*AN-FRIED DUCK BREASTS WITH LEEKS

S E R V E S
—— 4 ——

PREPARATION TIME
5 minutes
COOKING TIME
20 minutes

2 tablespoons olive oil
*4 leeks, halved lengthways
 and cut into 1-cm (½-in)
 pieces*
4 duck breasts, skinned
*4 tablespoons Noilly Prat or
 dry white wine*
*4 tablespoons hot chicken
 stock*
25 g (1 oz) unsalted butter
*Salt and freshly ground black
 pepper*

Duck breasts are relatively easy to find in the supermarket nowadays, but you might like to substitute large chicken breasts here instead. Though not as rich, they go equally well with leeks. You can – and, in my opinion, should – serve duck slightly rare. If you use chicken, make sure that it is cooked right through. The dish goes well with boiled new potatoes and a mixed green salad.

Heat the oil in a large frying-pan and sauté the leeks over a medium heat for 3–5 minutes until softened, but not browned. Remove from the pan with a slotted spoon and set aside. Raise the heat slightly and add the duck breasts to the pan. Cook for 5–8 minutes until browned on the outside, yet still pink on the inside. Lift the duck breasts out of the pan and keep warm.

Pour the Noilly Prat or wine into the pan and allow it to boil up and reduce slightly. Add the stock and reduce again. Stir in the butter until it has melted, return the leeks to the pan, and season to taste with salt and freshly ground black pepper.

Spoon the leeks and sauce onto hot plates, cut the duck breasts into thick diagonal slices and place on top of the leeks.

SMOKED TURKEY AND CABBAGE IN MANGO DRESSING

SERVES

—— 4 ——

T his is a really lovely salad. The dressing is thick with crushed fruit – just delightful. Use drained canned mango if you can't find fresh. I've used savoy cabbage because of its slightly nippy taste, which balances well with the mango, but other less strongly flavoured green or white cabbage could be used. Substitute cooked turkey for the smoked if you have some left over from a roast bird, or use sliced ham or cooked chicken instead.

———

Peel the peppers using a vegetable parer, then blanch them in boiling water for 2 minutes to soften. Drain the peppers, then refresh them under cold running water and pat dry with kitchen paper. Cut crossways into thin slivers and place in a large bowl with the turkey, cabbage and three-quarters of the mango.

Place the remaining mango in a food processor with the oil, vinegar and salt and freshly ground black pepper to taste. Whizz for a second or two to make a smooth purée, then pour over the turkey mixture. Toss together lightly and serve sprinkled with the chives.

INGREDIENTS

PREPARATION TIME
30 minutes
COOKING TIME
2 minutes

2 red peppers, de-seeded and
   quartered
350 g (12 oz) smoked
   turkey, sliced and cut into
   thin shreds
½ small savoy cabbage, very
   finely shredded
1 mango, peeled, stoned and
   diced
4 tablespoons olive oil
2 tablespoons white wine
   vinegar
Salt and freshly ground black
   pepper
2 tablespoons snipped fresh
   chives to garnish

MEAT

The trend nowadays is certainly to eat less meat, but most of us haven't given it up entirely. All but a few of the recipes are quite homely fare, with a bent towards Mediterranean, Middle Eastern and oriental flavours. I've included a few that are really cheap and cheerful winter food, while others are just a tad more summery.

Only one or two of the recipes are for beef, not only because I personally eat very little beef, but also because only the more expensive cuts can be cooked at any speed – and more to the point, who needs a recipe for grilled steak? Since I'm rather partial to lamb, and only slightly less so to pork, and because most cuts of both meats cook relatively quickly, there are more of these. However, especially in recipes using mince, the meats are interchangeable – in fact, even chicken or turkey mince could be used instead.

Whichever meat you use, but especially with pork, do go for those that are traditionally reared outside, where you can. The animals are better cared for, they are given fewer, if any, chemicals in their feed and, of course, the meat and the dishes that you cook taste better for it.

CURRIED LAMB WITH POTATOES

S E R V E S

—— 4 ——

INGREDIENTS

PREPARATION TIME
10 minutes
COOKING TIME
50 minutes

---

350 g (12 oz) baby new
potatoes, scrubbed and
halved
2 tablespoons sunflower oil
1 onion, peeled and finely
chopped
1 garlic clove, peeled and
crushed
450 g (1 lb) lamb neck fillet,
cut into 2.5-cm (1-in)
cubes
1 tablespoon curry powder
425-g (15-oz) can chopped
tomatoes
2 tablespoons tomato purée
225 g (8 oz) baby sweetcorn,
cut into 1-cm (½-in) pieces
Salt and freshly ground black
pepper

To get the best flavour make sure that the curry powder is well cooked, before you add the tomatoes. Use the new curry spice mixtures, that contain crushed rather than finely ground whole spices if you can, since they give a much better flavour too. If you have them in the vegetable drawer, substitute chunks of sweet potato, celeriac or parsnip for half of the potatoes. Serve the curry with rice, if you are especially hungry, and poppadoms.

Cook the potatoes in boiling salted water for 5 minutes, then drain. Meanwhile, heat the oil in a large pan and fry the onion and garlic for 5–8 minutes until softened and just beginning to brown. Stir in the lamb and cook, stirring occasionally, for 5 minutes until browned all over.

Stir in the curry powder and cook for 1 minute, then add the tomatoes, tomato purée, parboiled potatoes and bring to the boil. Cover and simmer for 20 minutes. Add the sweetcorn and salt and freshly ground black pepper and cook for 5–10 minutes more until the lamb and vegetables are tender.

CHORIZO SAUSAGE WITH CHERRY TOMATOES

S E R V E S
—— 4 ——

Cherry tomatoes are the sweetest and often the most flavoursome tomatoes. Kabanos or some other spicy sausage could be used in place of the chorizo. If you have only ordinary sausages leave them whole while you cook them with the onions, then lift them out of the pan and cut into thick diagonal slices before returning them to the pan with the tomatoes. Serve at once with chunks of crusty bread, pasta, tossed in a little olive oil, or some mashed potato.

———

Heat the oil in a large frying-pan and fry the onion and garlic over a medium heat, stirring occasionally, for about 5 minutes until softened. Add the chorizo to the pan, raise the heat slightly and fry for 5 minutes until the onion is beginning to brown. Add the tomatoes, parsley and salt and freshly ground black pepper to taste and cook for 2–3 minutes more until the tomatoes are hot and softened yet still holding their shape.

INGREDIENTS

PREPARATION TIME
8 minutes
COOKING TIME
12–15 minutes

3 tablespoons olive oil
1 onion, peeled and finely chopped
2 garlic cloves, peeled and crushed
350 g (12 oz) chorizo sausage, sliced
225 g (8 oz) cherry tomatoes, halved
4 tablespoons fresh chopped parsley
Salt and freshly ground black pepper

BEEF STRIPS STIR-FRIED WITH GINGER AND ORANGE

SERVES
—— 2–3 ——

PREPARATION TIME
10 minutes
COOKING TIME
5 minutes

2 tablespoons sunflower oil
1 garlic clove, peeled and
  crushed
5-cm (2-in) piece fresh root
  ginger, peeled and cut into
  thin slivers
4 carrots, halved lengthways
  and sliced thinly
450 g (1 lb) sirloin or fillet
  steak, cut into thin strips
1 tablespoon cornflour
150 ml (5 fl oz) beef stock
Grated rind and juice of 1
  orange
Salt and freshly ground black
  pepper

Because this cooks so fast, the beef really has to be the best, though rump steak, cut across the grain, would do at a push. Don't overcook it though or it will begin to toughen up. You can serve this simple dish just as it is with boiled or fried rice, or if you'd prefer to make it a bit more substantial or to stretch it to serve four, toss in a handful or two of mangetout and about eight baby sweetcorn, halved lengthways, with the carrots.

Heat the oil in a large frying-pan or wok over a medium heat, add the garlic, ginger and carrots and fry for 1 minute, stirring all the time. Raise the heat, tip in the beef strips and stir-fry for 2–3 minutes. Blend the cornflour with the stock and pour into the pan or wok with the orange rind and juice and cook for a few seconds until boiling and thickened. Season to taste with salt and freshly ground black pepper and serve at once.

GRILLED MARINATED PORK WITH SPICY PLUM SAUCE

SERVES
— 4 —

If you are organized and know today what you are going to cook tomorrow – and have the ingredients to hand – then prepare the marinade the night before so that the chops can marinate overnight. Although the preparation time looks long, because of the marinating, the dish is incredibly quick to put together. Depending on the sweetness of the plums, you may need to add a little sugar to the sauce, taste it before you serve and add a teaspoonful or two, if it needs it.

Place the pork steaks in a bowl. Scatter over the shallot or onion, then pour over the wine. Add the ginger, cinnamon, nutmeg and add salt and freshly ground black pepper and leave to marinate at room temperature for 20 minutes, or cover and place in the fridge overnight.

When you are ready to cook, lift the pork out of the marinade and pat dry on kitchen paper. Grill for 8–10 minutes, turning once until browned on the outside and cooked through.

While the pork is cooking place the marinade in a pan with the plums and cook over a high heat until the plums are tender and the marinade has reduced by half. Stir in the knob of butter until it melts, then serve hot with the pork.

INGREDIENTS

PREPARATION TIME
30 minutes
COOKING TIME
10 minutes

4 pork steaks, about 125 g (5 oz) each
1 shallot or ½ small onion, peeled and finely chopped
300 ml (10 fl oz) dry white wine
2.5-cm (1-in) piece fresh root ginger, peeled and finely grated
A pinch each of ground cinnamon and freshly grated nutmeg
Salt and freshly ground black pepper
175 g (6 oz) plums, quartered and stoned
Knob of butter

*H*ERBY HAMBURGERS TOPPED WITH BLUE CHEESE BUTTER

S E R V E S
—— 4 ——

PREPARATION TIME
10 minutes
COOKING TIME
10 minutes

350 g (12 oz) minced beef
1 garlic clove, peeled and crushed
1 teaspoon Dijon or wholegrain mustard
2 tablespoons each fresh chopped parsley, thyme and oregano
2 tablespoons sunflower oil
50 g (2 oz) butter
50 g (2 oz) blue Stilton cheese
Salt and freshly ground black pepper

I prefer to use Stilton for this butter, the lovely creamy texture and flavour is perfect with the savoury hamburgers. Put them in a toasted bun to eat on the hop, or serve on their own with a tomato salad and some crisps. You could, of course, just serve the hamburgers without the butter.

Mix together the beef, garlic, mustard, herbs and seasoning to taste; do this either in a food processor, whizzing it in short bursts until everything is just mixed, or in a bowl with one hand (which is a bit messier, but works well and, I think, makes a less dense hamburger into the bargain).

Turn the mixture on to a board, divide into 4 equal amounts and form into 2-cm (¾-in) thick rounds. Heat the oil in a large heavy-based frying-pan and fry the burgers for 3–5 minutes on each side until well browned on the outside and only just still pink on the inside.

While the hamburgers are cooking, beat together the butter and Stilton in a small bowl with a little salt and freshly ground black pepper to taste. Serve the burgers at once, topped with a dollop of the blue cheese butter.

HAM AND BROAD BEANS WITH PUFF PASTRY CRUSTS

SERVES

—— 4 ——

This dish is incredibly simple; you can use left-over ham from a home-cooked joint or slices bought from the deli counter, however, good-quality canned ham is really quite delicious prepared this way too.

Cook the beans in boiling salted water for 3–5 minutes until tender. Drain and refresh with cold water. Pre-heat the oven to gas mark 6, 200°C (400°F).

Roll the pastry out thinly to a rectangle, cut into 8 and, using a sharp knife, mark the tops lightly in a criss-cross pattern. Brush the pastry with egg or milk and bake for 10–12 minutes until the pastry is golden brown and well risen.

Meanwhile, make the sauce. Melt the butter in a pan, then stir in the flour and cook over a low heat for 1 minute. Remove from the heat and gradually stir in the milk, then return the pan to the heat and cook, stirring constantly, until the sauce is boiling, thickened and smooth. Add the parsley and season to taste with salt and freshly ground black pepper. Stir in the beans and ham and leave to simmer gently until the pastry is ready.

Serve the bean and ham mixture with the pastry squares accompanied with a light salad or some broccoli, or you can eat it on its own.

INGREDIENTS

PREPARATION TIME
6 minutes
COOKING TIME
15 minutes

225 g (8 oz) frozen broad beans
175 g (6 oz) ready-made puff pastry
Beaten egg or a little milk to glaze
225–350 g (8–12 oz) ham, cut in thick slices

FOR THE SAUCE
40 g (1 ½ oz) butter
40 g (1 ½ oz) plain flour
450 ml (15 fl oz) milk
4 tablespoons chopped fresh parsley
Salt and freshly ground black pepper

PAN-FRIED LAMB WITH PESTO AND PLUM TOMATOES

SERVES

—— 4 ——

Ready-made pesto from a jar is just fine in this dish, but if you have more time you could make your own using the recipe on page 85. I like to use the meaty chops cut from the fillet end of the leg, but chump chops are fine, or you could use little round noisettes, in which case you'd need two or even three per person. They only need to be cooked for 2–3 minutes on each side before you add the pesto and tomatoes. Delicious served with sautéed potatoes.

Heat the oil in a large frying-pan and fry the onion and garlic for 5 minutes, stirring occasionally, until softened. Add the chops and fry for 3–4 minutes on each side. Add the pesto, tomatoes and seasoning to taste. Cook for 2–3 minutes until the tomatoes have softened and the chops are cooked.

INGREDIENTS

PREPARATION TIME
5 minutes
COOKING TIME
15 minutes

2 tablespoons olive oil
1 small onion, peeled and
  finely chopped
1 garlic clove, peeled and
  crushed
4 leg of lamb chops, about
  175 g (6 oz) each
3 tablespoons pesto
225 g (8 oz) plum or other
  firm tomatoes, sliced
Salt and freshly ground black
  pepper

Baked lamb chops with tomatoes, green pepper and courgettes

S E R V E S

—— 4 ——

This is lovely warming winter fare, the sauce is full of flavour and would also be good with pork chops or braising steak instead of lamb. Pork will cook in about the same time, but you may have to leave braising steak to cook for up to 30 minutes more. You could always transfer the meat and sauce to a covered casserole, if that is easier, and bake in the oven at gas mark 5, 190°C (375°F).

Trim any fat from the chops and dip both sides of the meat in the seasoned flour. Heat the oil in a large sauté pan and brown the chops over a high heat, then remove the chops from the pan and set aside.

Add the onion, garlic and pepper to the pan, reduce the heat and fry for about 5 minutes until softened. Stir in the tomatoes and tomato purée, then return the chops to the pan, cover and bring to the boil. Reduce the heat and simmer for 25 minutes. Stir in the courgettes and cook for 5–10 minutes until the lamb is tender and the sauce reduced and thick. Taste the sauce and add extra salt and freshly ground black pepper, if necessary.

INGREDIENTS

PREPARATION TIME
10 minutes
COOKING TIME
45 minutes

4 lamb chump chops, about 150 g (5 oz) each
1 tablespoon flour seasoned with salt and freshly ground black pepper
2 tablespoons olive oil
1 onion, peeled and finely sliced
1 garlic clove, peeled and crushed
1 green pepper, de-seeded, quartered and finely sliced
225-g (8-oz) can chopped tomatoes
2 tablespoons tomato purée
4 small courgettes, thickly sliced diagonally

LEMONY LAMB FILLET WITH SPRING ONIONS

SERVES

— 4 —

Fresh lemon grass, which is available in ethnic shops as well as some large supermarkets, will give this dish a wonderfully aromatic, exotic flavour. Use just half a stalk, in place of the lemon rind. Chop it very finely and add to the pan with the ginger. Stir-fry oil is a ready-bottled mixture of sesame and chilli oils which gives it a lovely hot flavour. You could use pork fillet in place of the lamb, if you prefer.

Heat the oil in a frying-pan, add the ginger, garlic and lemon rind and fry for 1 minute. Add the lamb and fry for 3–4 minutes, stirring occasionally, until browned. Toss in the spring onions and cook for a minute or so more. Reduce the heat, then add the wine and yoghurt or soured cream, season to taste with salt and freshly ground black pepper and stir well. Serve at once.

INGREDIENTS

PREPARATION TIME
5 minutes
COOKING TIME
10 minutes

2 tablespoons stir-fry oil or sunflower oil

2.5-cm (1-in) piece of fresh root ginger, peeled and finely grated

1 garlic clove, peeled and crushed

Finely grated rind of 1 lemon

550 g (1 ¼ lb) lamb neck fillet, cut into short strips

6 spring onions, finely sliced

4 tablespoons dry white wine

5 tablespoons strained Greek yoghurt or soured cream

Salt and freshly ground black pepper

BAKED PORK STEAKS WITH APPLES AND HONEY

SERVES
— 4 —

Five-spice powder is used a lot in Chinese cooking. It is a mixture of anise pepper, fennel seed, cassia (which tastes like cinnamon), star anise and cloves. The combined flavour is quite powerful, almost liquoricey, yet this is almost undetectable when used in small quantities. A mixture of ground cinnamon and cloves could be used instead. You could serve this dish with plain noodles and a crisp salad of Chinese leaves, sliced water chestnuts and beansprouts.

Pre-heat the oven to gas mark 4, 180°C (350°F).

Heat the oil in a shallow, flameproof casserole and fry the chops for 2–3 minutes on each side until well browned – cook them 2 at a time if your casserole isn't large enough to fit 4. Sprinkle on the five-spice powder and some seasoning, then add the wine and bring to the boil. Cover the casserole, transfer to the oven, and bake for 45 minutes.

Cut the apples into quarters and remove the cores, then remove the casserole from the oven and arrange the apple quarters around the meat. Pour over the orange juice and honey and return to the oven, uncovered, for 10–15 minutes until the apples and the pork are tender; baste the apples and meat occasionally with the juices.

INGREDIENTS

PREPARATION TIME
10 minutes
COOKING TIME
1 hour

4 thick pork steaks, about
175 g (6 oz) each
2 tablespoons olive oil
1 teaspoon five-spice powder
Salt and freshly ground black
pepper
150 ml (5 fl oz) dry white
wine
4 small dessert apples,
quartered and cored
Juice of 1 orange
2 tablespoons clear honey

SAUSAGE, ONION AND POTATO BAKE

S E R V E S

—— 4 ——

PREPARATION TIME
15 minutes
COOKING TIME
1 hour 45 minutes

1 tablespoon sunflower oil
225 g (8 oz) herby sausages
6–8 medium potatoes, sliced
2 onions, peeled and finely
*   sliced*

FOR THE SAUCE
50 g (2 oz) butter
50 g (2 oz) plain flour
600 ml (1 pint) milk
1 teaspoon Dijon or
*   wholegrain mustard*
Pinch of freshly grated
*   nutmeg*
Salt and freshly ground black
*   pepper*

This is fairly cheap and cheerful fare, the kind of food I used to cook when I was a student. It's one of the few recipes in the book that has a lengthy cooking time, but it is speedy to put together and, for something that costs so little, the flavour is really rather good. Grill the sausages instead of frying them, if you prefer, and use thick-cut back bacon, or pieces of left-over ham instead of the sausages for a change.

Pre-heat the oven to gas mark 5, 190°C (375°F).

Heat the oil in a large frying-pan and fry the sausages for about 5 minutes until well browned. Meanwhile, make the sauce; melt the butter in a small pan, stir in the flour and cook over a low heat for 1 minute. Remove the pan from the heat and gradually stir in the milk. Return the pan to the heat and cook, stirring all the time, until the sauce is boiling, thickened and smooth. Then stir in the mustard, nutmeg and salt and freshly ground black pepper to taste.

Cut the cooked sausages into chunks and layer them with the potatoes and onions in a large, lightly greased casserole, then pour over the sauce. Shake the casserole from side to side until the sauce runs down to the bottom and cover with a lid. Bake for 1 hour, then remove the lid and bake for 15–20 minutes more until the potatoes and onion are tender and the top is browned.

Meatballs with Tomato Sauce

S E R V E S
—— 4 ——

This is a great dish to serve for family meals since it appeals to children of all ages and adults like it too. Incidentally it also freezes well so, if you have the time, make up double the recipe and freeze half before you do the final cooking. Once defrosted you would then simmer the dish for the final 20 minutes. Serve with pasta shells or garlicky mashed potatoes.

———

Make the sauce first. Heat the oil in a large shallow pan and fry the onion, carrot and celery for 3 minutes. Stir in the bacon and cook for 3–5 minutes more until the bacon is cooked. Stir in the tomatoes, tomato purée, wine, oregano or parsley and salt and freshly ground black pepper to taste. Bring to the boil, then reduce the heat and leave to simmer gently while you make the meatballs.

In a large bowl, mix together the minced lamb, garlic, parsley, beaten eggs, breadcrumbs and plenty of seasoning. Using damp hands, form the mixture into 16 balls. Heat the oil in a frying-pan and fry the meatballs in batches until browned all over. Lift out of the pan with a slotted spoon, drain on kitchen paper, then add to the tomato sauce. Cover and simmer gently for 20 minutes.

INGREDIENTS

PREPARATION TIME
35 minutes
COOKING TIME
20 minutes

450 g (1 lb) minced lamb
2 garlic cloves, peeled and crushed
2 tablespoons chopped fresh parsley
2 eggs, beaten
100 g (4 oz) fresh breadcrumbs
Salt and freshly ground black pepper
4 tablespoons olive oil
FOR THE SAUCE
2 tablespoons olive oil
1 onion, peeled and chopped
1 carrot, chopped
1 celery stalk, chopped
100 g (4 oz) streaky bacon rashers, chopped
2 × 425-g (15-oz) cans chopped tomatoes
2 tablespoons tomato purée
4 tablespoons dry white wine
2 teaspoons chopped fresh oregano or parsley
Salt and freshly ground black pepper

HAM AND TURKEY WITH A SPICY RAISIN SAUCE

SERVES
—— 4 ——

PREPARATION TIME
15 minutes
COOKING TIME
20 minutes

25 g (1 oz) unsalted butter
225–350 g (8–12 oz)
  cooked ham, thickly sliced
225–350 g (8–12 oz)
  cooked turkey, thickly
  sliced

FOR THE SAUCE
4 tablespoons raisins
¼ teaspoon ground cloves
¼ teaspoon ground cinnamon
1-cm (½-in) piece fresh root
  ginger, peeled and finely
  grated
Grated rind and juice of 1
  orange and 1 lemon
1 tablespoon white wine
  vinegar
1 tablespoon dark muscovado
  sugar
1 teaspoon cornflour, mixed
  with a little water

This is a great way to use up the left-overs from the Christmas roast, but you could just buy ready-sliced meats from the deli counter. Remember that you are only heating through the meats, since they are already cooked, so don't overdo the frying. It is equally good with all ham or all turkey, but the combination of the two is quite good. Left-over pork could be cooked in the same way.

Make the sauce first, place all the ingredients in a pan and bring to the boil, stirring all the time. Simmer gently for 5 minutes. Meanwhile, melt the butter in a large frying-pan and fry the ham and turkey slices over a high heat until browned and hot. Serve at once with the sauce poured on top.

Char-grilled lamb with mediterranean vegetables

S E R V E S

—— 4 ——

Use a combination of pepper colours if you can, super-markets often sell mixed bags of three different kinds. As for the tomatoes, the medium-sized Provençale tomatoes available in the summer are good and tasty but plum tomatoes or beefsteak tomatoes would be fine too. If the beefsteak tomatoes are particularly large, then two would probably be quite enough.

———

Arrange the lamb and vegetables in a large glass dish and tuck the thyme sprigs in amongst them. Mix together the oil and wine with salt and plenty of freshly ground black pepper and pour over the lamb and vegetables. Leave to marinate at room temperature for 20 minutes, then lift the lamb and vegetables out of the marinade and arrange them in one layer on a grill pan rack. Grill for 10–15 minutes, until the chops and veg-etables are tender and everything is nicely browned, turning them occasionally. Serve hot, with any juices from the pan and sprinkled with the chopped parsley and some slices of warmed, floury ciabatta bread.

INGREDIENTS

PREPARATION TIME
30 minutes
COOKING TIME
10–15 minutes

4 leg of lamb chops
2–3 red, yellow, green or orange peppers, de-seeded and quartered lengthways
4 large flat mushrooms, stalks trimmed
4 large tomatoes, halved
1 small aubergine, thickly sliced
2 small courgettes, halved lengthways
A few sprigs of thyme
2 tablespoons chopped fresh parsley to garnish

FOR THE MARINADE
2 tablespoons olive oil
150 ml (5 fl oz) red wine
Salt and freshly ground black pepper

LAMB TIKKA

SERVES

—— 4 ——

This isn't too hot and, possibly because mini kebabs are fun to eat, children like it too. If you can, prepare the marinade and lamb in the morning, or even the night before, to allow the lamb to absorb the spicy flavours. Serve with extra yoghurt, a leafy salad and rice or noodles.

Trim any fat from the lamb and cut into 2.5-cm (1-in) cubes. Place the lamb cubes in a large bowl, then add the spice mix, garlic, yoghurt and salt to taste and mix together thoroughly. Leave to marinate at room temperature for 20 minutes, stirring occasionally.

Thread 5 or 6 cubes loosely on to each of 12 short skewers, then grill the lamb for 10–12 minutes until well browned on the outside and still just slightly pink in the middle.

INGREDIENTS

PREPARATION TIME
30 minutes
COOKING TIME
10–15 minutes

750 g (1 ½ lb) boneless leg of
   lamb
1 tablespoon tandoori spice
   mix
2 garlic cloves, peeled and
   crushed
4 tablespoons natural
   yoghurt
Salt

RED HOT RIBS

S E R V E S

—— 4 ——

The ribs take only a few mintues to get ready, before they go into the oven for an hour and a half, which I know isn't very quick, but it is easy. If you are serving the ribs to children, reduce the chilli powder to ½ teaspoon. Serve them on their own and make a big leafy salad or some fried rice to eat afterwards. Provide everyone with big cloth napkins and small bowls of warm water to rinse their sticky fingers.

Pre-heat the oven to gas mark 5, 190°C (375°F).

Put all the ingredients, except the ribs, in a bowl and mix together thoroughly. Put the ribs in a very large bowl, pour over the sauce and turn the ribs to coat thoroughly. Spread out the ribs in a large baking tin and cook uncovered for 1½ hours, until the pork is very tender, turning the ribs over once or twice. Serve hot with the thick syrupy sauce from the baking tin, poured over the top.

INGREDIENTS

PREPARATION TIME
5 minutes
COOKING TIME
1 hour 30 minutes

2 garlic cloves, peeled and
crushed
1 teaspoon chilli powder
½ teaspoon ground ginger
3 tablespoons clear honey
2 tablespoons light
muscovado sugar
4 tablespoons tomato ketchup
4 tablespoons white or red
wine vinegar
2 tablespoons soy sauce
2 tablespoons barbecue sauce
1 tablespoon chilli sauce
1.5 kg (3 lb) pork spare ribs
Salt and freshly ground black
pepper

KASHMIR PORK BALLS ON SKEWERS

SERVES
—— 4 ——

Pale yellow gram or besan flour is available in Indian food shops. It's the basis for all sorts of traditional dishes and has a distinctive, sweet flavour, but there's no need to buy it specially for this dish, plain flour will suffice. The aromatic spice mix called garam masala usually includes cardamom, cinnamon and cloves but you could get away with adding a tandoori spice mixture or even curry powder instead. These are quite good cold too, so you could cook them to take on a picnic.

Place the pork, flour, spices, ginger, coriander, yoghurt, breadcrumbs and salt to taste in a bowl and mix together thoroughly – use your hand, it's by far the easiest way. Tip the mixture out on to a board and divide into 20 equal portions. Roll into small balls in the palm of your hands, then thread on to 4 long skewers. Grill for 10–12 minutes until the pork balls are cooked through and browned, turning the skewers occasionally.

While the pork balls are cooking, make the raita: mix together the yoghurt, cucumber, mint, coriander and salt and freshly ground black pepper to taste. Serve the pork balls hot with the raita.

INGREDIENTS

PREPARATION TIME
20 minutes
COOKING TIME
12 minutes

450 g (1 lb) minced pork
1 tablespoon gram flour or
    plain flour
2 tablespoons garam masala
1 teaspoon ground cardamom
    seeds
Pinch of cayenne pepper
2.5-cm (1-in) piece fresh
    root ginger, peeled and
    finely grated
2 tablespoons chopped fresh
    coriander
4 tablespoons strained Greek
    yoghurt
50 g (2 oz) fresh
    breadcrumbs
Salt

FOR THE RAITA
225 g (8 oz) strained Greek
    yoghurt
¼ cucumber, diced
1 tablespoon chopped fresh
    mint
1 tablespoon chopped fresh
    coriander
Salt and freshly ground black
    pepper

Opposite: SALMON, TOMATO AND EGG FLAT TART (*page 78*)

Overleaf: HAM AND BROAD BEANS WITH PUFF PASTRY CRUST (*page 55*) *and* CHEF'S SALAD WITH EGGS AND BLUE CHEESE (*page 76*)

BLACK PUDDING WITH APPLES

S E R V E S
—— 3–4 ——

I first ate this dish on holiday in Brittany a few years ago. It's one of those recipes that initially sounds a bit strange but if you like black pudding it is well worth trying. The French black puddings, known as *boudin noir*, have a particularly good texture and flavour. It is possible to get good black pudding here from independent butchers, the large pre-packed black puddings that are sold cut in thick slices will do as a last resort. Some recipes include a little cider or a splash of Calvados to the pan at the end to bubble up into a sauce, but it is delicious without. As for the apples, choose something crisp (so they hold their shape) with a good flavour, such as Cox's Pippin, Gala or Russet varieties.

Heat the oil in a large frying-pan and fry the black pudding over a fairly high heat for 5 minutes, stirring occasionally, until just cooked through and slightly crisp on the outside. Add the apple quarters and cook for 5–8 minutes more until the apples are tender and beginning to brown. Season to taste with black pepper and serve at once with chunks of French bread.

INGREDIENTS

PREPARATION TIME
10 minutes
COOKING TIME
10 minutes

2 tablespoons olive oil
750g (1 ½ lb) black pudding,
  cut into thick chunks
4 dessert apples, quartered
  and cored
Freshly ground black pepper

Opposite: PASTA WITH CAULIFLOWER AND CHORIZO (*page 99*)

EGGS

The original convenience food, eggs are almost omnipresent – there are surely half a dozen lurking in even the most poorly stocked fridge. Eggs on their own are perhaps the quickest cooked meal you can make, which is why they are so popular at breakfast time. And one would have to say that the traditional English breakfast of two eggs, a couple of slices of bacon and four tomato halves, fried in olive oil instead of the original dripping, makes a very speedy and very tasty supper – and with a slice or two of wholemeal toast, it is positively healthy too!

When combined with other ingredients, eggs can be turned into really fabulous fast meals. The Mediterranean way of making an omelette with vegetables is just wonderful – and unlike an ordinary omelette, tastes as good cold.

The biggest, and most pleasant, surprise when I wrote this chapter was the salads. If boiled eggs and lettuce doesn't sound all that exciting to you, think again and try them out. I tested the recipes in the depths of the winter, yet it didn't matter that these two dishes were cold – they were, even though I say it myself, simply delicious.

PIPÉRADE

S E R V E S

—— 4 ——

INGREDIENTS

PREPARATION TIME
5 minutes
COOKING TIME
10 minutes

225 g (8 oz) plum tomatoes,
*   peeled and roughly*
*   chopped*
25 g (1 oz) butter
1 tablespoon olive oil
1 onion, peeled and finely
*   chopped*
1 tablespoon fresh oregano,
*   chopped*
6 eggs, beaten
Salt and freshly ground black
*   pepper*

Pipérade is a cross between scrambled eggs and an ome-lette. In the Basque region of south-west France where this recipe originates, it is often served with grilled or fried ham, in particular slices of jambon de Bayonne. To make the dish more substantial, you could mix in about 100 g (4 oz) diced cooked ham, mushrooms or cooked, peeled prawns at the same time as the tomatoes. Plum tomatoes have a good strong flavour and firm flesh, but if they are not available use cherry tomatoes which don't need to be peeled, just halved.

Place the chopped tomatoes in a sieve to drain while you heat the butter and oil in a frying-pan. Cook the onion over a low to medium heat until softened and just beginning to brown. Add the tomatoes and oregano and cook for 2–3 minutes until heated through. Season the eggs with salt and freshly ground black pepper and pour them into the pan. Stir gently over a low heat until the eggs are just set, yet still creamy, then serve at once with crusty bread.

TORTILLA

S E R V E S

— 4 —

This traditional potato and onion omelette, with slight regional variations, is made all over Spain. Choose firm, but not waxy potatoes, such as Maris Piper, Romano or Wilja. You do need a good, big, heavy, non-stick frying-pan for this recipe. The tricky bit is turning the omelette over to cook the other side. You can just cheat: put the omelette, still in the pan, under the grill to cook the top. You can serve it hot or cold, cut into wedges.

Heat the oil in a large, non-stick frying-pan and fry the potatoes for 2–3 minutes, stirring until well coated with oil. Add the onion and fry over a medium heat for 15–20 minutes until the potatoes and onion are cooked, but not browned.

Beat the eggs in a large bowl with salt and freshly ground black pepper to taste. Drain off any excess oil from the potatoes and onions, then tip them into the beaten eggs and mix well. Return the pan to the heat and pour in the egg mixture. Cook on a low heat, pulling the cooked mixture from the sides into the centre to let the raw egg run to the sides. As it cooks, keep the depth of the tortilla fairly even.

When the tortilla is almost set, leave it to cook undisturbed for a few minutes to brown the base and sides, then turn the tortilla over – place a large plate on top of the pan and holding both together firmly, turn the tortilla quickly upside-down on to the plate. Slide it straight back into the pan and cook until the other side is golden brown. Serve hot or cold.

INGREDIENTS

PREPARATION TIME
10 minutes
COOKING TIME
30 minutes

4 tablespoons olive oil
450 g (1 lb) old potatoes, peeled and cut into 1-cm (½-in) chunks
1 large Spanish onion, peeled and chopped
6 eggs, beaten
Salt and freshly ground black pepper

CHEF'S SALAD WITH EGGS AND BLUE CHEESE

SERVES

— 4 —

This salad needs some crisp lettuce. Iceberg, cos lettuce or Chinese leaves are all good either on their own or as a mixture of two or all three. I'd avoid Danish Blue for the dressing as it has too harsh a flavour and add some crumbled Stilton, Dunsyre Blue, Roquefort or Gorgonzola. Serve with hot French bread spread with garlic and herb butter.

Place the eggs in a pan of water and bring to the boil. Turn down the heat and simmer for 7 minutes.

While the eggs are cooking, place all the other salad ingredients in a large bowl. Then make the dressing: mix together the vinegar, olive oil and salt and freshly ground black pepper, then beat into the mayonnaise until smooth. Stir in the blue cheese and set aside.

When the eggs are cooked, drain and leave to cool in cold water, then shell, cut into wedges and add to the salad. Pour over the dressing and toss lightly to mix. Serve at once.

INGREDIENTS

PREPARATION TIME
15 minutes
COOKING TIME
10 minutes

4 eggs
1 crisp lettuce (iceberg, cos lettuce or Chinese leaves), finely shredded
½ cucumber, diced
1 red, orange or yellow pepper, de-seeded and diced
4 celery stalks, sliced
200-g (7-oz) can sweetcorn, drained
150 g (5 oz) mixed sprouted seeds and beans
100 g (4 oz) salami, sliced thickly and cut into thin strips
2 tablespoons chopped fresh parsley

FOR THE DRESSING
2 tablespoons white wine vinegar
5 tablespoons olive oil
Salt and freshly ground black pepper
150 ml (5 fl oz) mayonnaise
100 g (4 oz) blue cheese, crumbled

OMELETTE WITH FRESH PARSLEY

S E R V E S

—— 2 ——

The best-tasting eggs in our supermarkets are the relatively new 'fourgrain' eggs laid by hens fed purely on cereals – they cost a bit more, but taste a whole lot better than battery eggs. The hens are having a better time too, since they are kept in barns or percheries instead of tiny cages and have the freedom to roam around.

You could add some grated cheese, cooked prawns or chopped bacon with the parsley.

Beat the eggs in a bowl with 1 tablespoon of cold water per egg. Add salt and freshly ground black pepper to taste. Heat a 17-cm (7-in) omelette pan, drop in the butter and let it melt – the pan needs to be hot but not so hot that the butter browns before it melts.

Pour in the beaten egg and cook over a fairly high heat. Use a fork to pull the egg from the outside to the centre as it cooks, letting the raw egg flow on to the base of the pan. When the egg is almost all set, leave the omelette to cook undisturbed for a moment or two to allow the base to brown – the surface of the omelette should still be soft, almost runny. Remember that it will continue to cook while you finish and serve it. Scatter over the parsley, flip the omelette in half, tip it out on to a heated plate and serve at once.

INGREDIENTS

PREPARATION TIME
3 minutes
COOKING TIME
4–5 minutes

4–6 eggs
Salt and freshly ground black
  pepper
25 g (1 oz) butter
4 tablespoons chopped fresh
  parsley

SALMON, TOMATO AND EGG FLAT TART

SERVES

— 4 —

PREPARATION TIME
15 minutes
COOKING TIME
45 minutes

*225 g (8 oz) ready-made
    shortcrust pastry, thawed
    if frozen*
2 tablespoons olive oil
*1 shallot or ½ small onion,
    peeled and finely chopped*
*1 garlic clove, peeled and
    crushed*
*100 g (4 oz) tomatoes, cut
    into wedges*
*25 g (1 oz) sun-dried
    tomatoes in olive oil,
    drained and chopped*
*225-g (8-oz) can salmon,
    drained*
*Salt and freshly ground black
    pepper*
2 eggs, beaten
*120 ml (4 fl oz) double
    cream*
*1 tablespoon basil leaves,
    shredded*
*25 g (1 oz) Parmesan
    cheese, pared into thin
    shavings*

N ot a quiche, and not a pizza either, but something in between. The base is shortcrust pastry, but it's easier than a flan, because there is no flan case to make. It could, of course, be made without the sun-dried tomatoes, but their strong, sweet flavour is a wonderful addition.

Pre-heat the oven to gas mark 5, 190°C (375°F).

Roll out the pastry to a 30-cm (12-inch) round. Damp the edge and turn in all the way round to create a little wall about 1 cm (½ in) high. Prick the pastry lightly with a fork, place on a baking sheet and chill for 10 minutes.

Heat the oil in a frying-pan and fry the onion and garlic over a low heat for 5–8 minutes until softened and just beginning to brown. Stir in the fresh and sun-dried tomatoes, then remove the pan from the heat. Flake the salmon and stir in lightly; add salt and freshly ground black pepper to taste.

Spread the tomato mixture over the pastry, then whisk together the eggs and cream with salt and freshly ground black pepper to taste and pour carefully over the tomato mixture. Bake for about 30 minutes until the pastry is crisp and golden and the egg mixture lightly set. Scatter the basil and Parmesan cheese over the top and serve at once.

RÖSTI WITH TWO FRIED EGGS – SUNNY SIDE UP

SERVES

—— 1 ——

I suppose this is the Swiss equivalent of egg and chips. Since the potatoes need to be cooked a day ahead, either you have to be organized and cook them the day before, or make it when there are left-over potatoes to use up. The potatoes must be firm and waxy, like new potatoes or those knobbly little potatoes sold in supermarkets as salad potatoes. I have made the recipe for one but you could very easily double, or even quadruple, the quantities.

Place the grated potatoes in a bowl and season with salt and freshly ground black pepper. Heat 15 g (½ oz) of the butter and 1 teaspoon of the oil in a small non-stick frying-pan. Add the potatoes and press down with the back of a wooden spoon to make a cake. Cook over a medium heat for about 15 minutes until the base is crisp and golden brown. Cover the pan with a plate, then turn both pan and plate over. Holding them tightly, remove the pan, return it to the heat and add half of the remaining butter and the remaining oil. Slide the rösti back into the pan and cook the other side for about 10 minutes.

A few minutes before the rösti is ready, heat the remaining butter in another frying-pan. Break in the eggs and season to taste with salt and freshly ground black pepper. Fry them over a medium heat until just set, spooning the hot butter over the tops to cook them too. Serve the rösti hot, with the eggs, sunny side up, on top.

INGREDIENTS

PREPARATION TIME
10 minutes
COOKING TIME
25 minutes

225 g (8 oz) cooked, firm waxy potatoes, coarsely grated
Salt and freshly ground black pepper
40 g (1 ½ oz) butter
2 teaspoons sunflower oil
2 eggs

OMELETTE ARNOLD BENNETT

S E R V E S
—— 2 ——

T his classic omelette is named after the novelist, Arnold Bennett, who ate it at the Savoy Hotel in London. Add some extra Parmesan cheese if you like the flavour and serve with buttered, toasted muffins. For the very best flavour, use an Arbroath smokie instead of smoked haddock fillet – you'll need about 350 g (12 oz) to allow for the head, bones and skin.

INGREDIENTS

PREPARATION TIME
5 minutes
COOKING TIME
25 minutes

---

225 g (8 oz) smoked
  haddock fillet
150 ml (5 fl oz) milk
120 ml (4 fl oz) double
  cream
4 eggs
Salt and freshly ground black
  pepper
25 g (1 oz) unsalted butter
25 g (1 oz) Parmesan
  cheese, grated

Place the haddock in a large frying-pan and pour over the milk and 150 ml (5 fl oz) water. Bring to the boil, then reduce the heat and poach the haddock gently for 5 minutes. Leave until cool enough to handle, then lift out of the liquid with a slotted spoon and flake, removing the skin and bones. Place the haddock in a bowl and stir in all but 2 tablespoons of the cream. Set aside.

Beat together the eggs, salt and freshly ground black pepper and 6 tablespoons of cold water. Heat a 23-cm (9-in) omelette pan, then add the butter – the pan should be hot enough to melt the butter at once, but not to burn it. Pour in the egg mixture and cook over a medium heat. As the egg begins to set around the edge, pull it into the centre with a fork and allow the raw egg to run to the outside of the pan. Continue cooking until the omelette has just softly set and the underside is lightly golden.

Spoon the haddock mixture into the middle, leave to heat through for a minute or two, then fold the omelette in half and gently tip out of the pan on to a heated, flameproof serving dish. Pour over the reserved cream and scatter the Parmesan cheese on top. Brown under a hot grill, then serve at once.

SPINACH AND TOMATO EGGAH

SERVES
— 2 —

This is another big flat omelette, this time from the Middle East. It isn't turned, the top is browned under the grill. The finished eggah should be crisp and golden on the outside and soft and just barely set on the inside, so cook in a medium-sized, heavy-based frying-pan. Use fresh baby spinach instead of frozen when it is in season, you'll need about 450 g (1 lb). Wash it well, trim off the stalks and add the leaves to the cooked onion. Cook for a moment or two until the leaves wilt before adding the eggs.

———

Heat the oil in a non-stick frying-pan and cook the onion and garlic for 5 minutes, stirring occasionally, until softened but not brown. Meanwhile put the frozen spinach in a small pan with 4 tablespoons of water and cook for about 5 minutes until the spinach has thawed. Drain thoroughly and squeeze dry, then add to the onion mixture with the tomatoes.

Beat the eggs with the nutmeg and salt and freshly ground black pepper to taste, then pour them into the pan. Mix well and cook, covered, over a very low heat without stirring until the eggah sets. Place the pan under a hot grill to cook the top, then slide the eggah out of the pan on to a serving plate and cut into wedges. Serve hot or cold.

INGREDIENTS

PREPARATION TIME
5 minutes
COOKING TIME
15 minutes

2 tablespoons olive oil
1 onion, peeled and chopped
2 garlic cloves, peeled and crushed
225 g (8 oz) frozen chopped spinach
3 tomatoes, peeled and cut into wedges
4 eggs
¼ teaspoon freshly grated nutmeg
Salt and freshly ground black pepper

CAESAR SALAD

SERVES

—— 4 ——

This is a great salad, it is amazing that a few quite ordinary ingredients can taste so good! The lettuce needs to be absolutely dry before you add the dressing or the dressing won't stick and will just run off, down to the bottom of the bowl. The dressing traditionally has a raw egg in it, which you can beat in with the oil, if you like, but it is sensational as it is.

Place the eggs in a pan of cold water, bring to the boil, then simmer for 7 minutes. Drain, then cool under cold running water.

Meanwhile, grill the bacon until crisp and brown and, at the same time, heat the oil and butter together in a frying-pan and fry the bread cubes until crisp and golden. Drain the bacon and bread cubes on kitchen paper, then snip the bacon into thin strips with a pair of scissors and set aside. Shell the cooled eggs and cut into wedges.

Tear the lettuce into small pieces and place in a large salad bowl. Scatter the bacon and croûtons over the lettuce, then add the eggs and the anchovies.

Make the dressing: whisk together the vinegar, oil, mustard and garlic until well mixed, adding salt and freshly ground black pepper to taste. Then stir in the parsley. Pour over the salad just before serving and toss together gently. Scatter over the shavings of Parmesan cheese and serve at once.

INGREDIENTS

PREPARATION TIME
10 minutes
COOKING TIME
15 minutes

4 eggs
225 g (8 oz) smoked back
   bacon rashers
2 tablespoons olive oil
25 g (1 oz) butter
2 thick slices firm textured
   wholemeal bread, cut into
   cubes
1 large head cos lettuce,
   washed and dried well
50-g (2-oz) can anchovy
   fillets, drained and
   chopped
25 g (1 oz) Parmesan
   cheese, pared into thin
   shavings with a potato
   peeler

FOR THE DRESSING
2 tablespoons white wine
   vinegar
6 tablespoons olive oil
1 teaspoon Dijon mustard
2 garlic cloves, peeled and
   crushed
Salt and freshly ground black
   pepper
2 tablespoons finely chopped
   fresh parsley

PASTA

Fresh pasta is a relatively new addition to the supermarket chiller cabinet, but I'd have to say it is the one food that my family eat most. The wonderful thing about it is that it cooks so quickly – even from frozen the plain varieties take a maximum of 5 minutes, and the stuffed pastas take only 10 or 12 minutes.

There are lots of extremely quick and interesting ways of serving pasta, as the following recipes show. Yet you can make an instant supper just by tossing the pasta in a flavoursome olive oil and scattering over a handful of chopped herbs – basil is a favourite in our house – adding a spoonful or two of chopped sun-dried tomatoes (my husband's speciality) or mixing in some grated cheese; the children prefer plain Cheddar cheese, whereas I like freshly grated Parmesan. (By the way, if you have one of those dreadful tubs of dried Parmesan in the cupboard, then please throw it away and buy a chunk of the real thing.)

All you need with most pasta dishes is a simple salad and a slice or two of really good bread – the floury ciabatta that is available in most supermarkets, heated in the oven for a few minutes, is ideal. The only other accompaniment I'd suggest is a glass of slightly rustic red wine.

TAGLIATELLE WITH MUSHROOMS AND GARLIC

SERVES
— 4 —

There was a time when I would have specified button mushrooms for this recipe, but there is now such a wide variety of mushrooms, both cultivated and wild, for sale that it seems a shame to limit the choice. I'd still avoid large flat mushrooms which would make the sauce very dark and murky.

Cook the tagliatelle in plenty of boiling salted water until *al dente*; dried pasta will take about 10 minutes, fresh about 4–5 minutes.

While the pasta is cooking (or earlier if using fresh pasta), heat the oil and butter in a large pan. Add the mushrooms and garlic and fry for 3–5 minutes until the mushrooms are cooked. Stir in the flour and cook for 1 minute, then pour in the stock and Noilly Prat or wine and cook, stirring, until boiling and thickened. Stir in the tomato purée and seasoning and simmer gently for 2–3 minutes.

As soon as the pasta is cooked, drain at once in a colander. Transfer the tagliatelle to hot plates and pour over the sauce. Scatter the parsley over the top and serve at once.

INGREDIENTS

PREPARATION TIME
5 minutes
COOKING TIME
10–15 minutes

350 g (12 oz) fresh or dried
    tagliatelle
2 tablespoons olive oil
25 g (1 oz) butter
450 g (1 lb) mushrooms,
    sliced
1 garlic clove, peeled and
    crushed
1 tablespoon plain flour
150 ml (5 fl oz) chicken or
    vegetable stock
2 tablespoons Noilly Prat or
    dry white wine
2 tablespoons tomato purée
Salt and freshly ground black
    pepper
4 tablespoons chopped fresh
    parsley to garnish

PENNE
WITH PESTO

S E R V E S
—— 4 ——

B asil plants, which can be bought all year round in large supermarkets, grow quite successfully throughout the year on a sunny windowsill. Carefully nip off pairs of leaves, rather than chopping off whole branches and given time (and plenty of water) the plant will bush out and produce even more leaves.

Cook the penne in plenty of boiling salted water until *al dente*. This will take 8–10 minutes for dried pasta, 3–4 minutes for fresh.

Meanwhile, put the basil, garlic, pine kernels, oil and salt into a food processor and whizz to a fine paste, add the Parmesan and whizz again briefly.

As soon as the pasta is cooked, drain at once in a colander. Tip the penne back-into the pan, add the pesto sauce, butter and freshly ground black pepper and toss until the butter melts and mixes with the sauce. Serve at once, with bread if you are very hungry.

INGREDIENTS

PREPARATION TIME
5 minutes
COOKING TIME
10 minutes

450 g (1 lb) fresh or *dried pasta quills (penne)*
50 g (2 oz) basil leaves
2 garlic cloves, peeled and crushed
25 g (1 oz) pine kernels
4 tablespoons extra virgin olive oil
½ teaspoon salt
50 g (2 oz) Parmesan cheese, finely grated
25 g (1 oz) butter
Freshly ground black pepper

SPAGHETTI WITH CARBONARA SAUCE

S E R V E S
—— 4 ——

P asta really should be eaten as soon as it is cooked, and not set aside to wait for the sauce. Make sure the rest of the ingredients are prepared while it is cooking so they are ready to add. If you use fresh pasta (which cooks in only two or three minutes) in place of dried spaghetti, start the bacon cooking first, beat the eggs and have the water boiling ready to cook the pasta when the bacon is almost done. You'll still have time to grate the cheese and heat the plates while the pasta cooks.

———

Bring a large pan of salted water to the boil. Place the spaghetti in the pan and, as it softens, bend it round and push under the water with a wooden spoon. Cook until *al dente*; dried spaghetti will take about 10 minutes, fresh pasta 2–3 minutes.

While the pasta is cooking, fry the bacon in a large, heavy non-stick pan for 5 minutes until crisp and brown, then keep hot.

Beat together the eggs, cream or milk, Parmesan cheese and seasoning. Then when the spaghetti is cooked, drain in a colander and then tip it into the hot pan with the bacon. Pour in the egg mixture and stir gently over a very low heat for 2–3 minutes until the sauce thickens slightly. Serve at once with thick chunks of white crusty bread or ciabatta, the Italian olive oil bread.

INGREDIENTS

PREPARATION TIME
5 minutes
COOKING TIME
15 minutes

350 g (12 oz) fresh or dried spaghetti
350 g (12 oz) smoked bacon chops, cut into thick shreds
4 eggs
4 tablespoons single cream or milk
50 g (2 oz) Parmesan cheese, finely grated
Salt and freshly ground black pepper

Rigatoni with Gorgonzola Sauce

S E R V E S

—— 4 ——

Gorgonzola has a wonderfully rich piquant flavour and makes a really speedy, delicious sauce for pasta. You could make a crisp salad of small mixed lettuce leaves and herbs such as chervil and flat leaf parsley to serve with it. Add a dressing made with olive oil, a little walnut oil if you have it, and balsamic or white wine vinegar and toss in a handful of chopped, toasted walnuts.

Cook the pasta in plenty of boiling salted water until *al dente*, about 10 minutes.

While the pasta is cooking, place the cheese in a large pan with the oil and butter and melt over a very low heat, stirring gently. As soon as it has melted, stir in the pistachio nuts, cream, brandy and seasoning and heat through.

When the pasta is cooked, drain in a colander. Tip the pasta into the sauce, stir well and serve at once, sprinkled with the Parmesan cheese.

INGREDIENTS

PREPARATION TIME
5 minutes
COOKING TIME
15 minutes

350 g (12 oz) rigatoni
225 g (8 oz) Gorgonzola
  cheese, diced
4 tablespoons olive oil
50 g (2 oz) butter
100 g (4 oz) shelled
  pistachio nuts, chopped
150 ml (5 fl oz) single cream
2 tablespoons brandy
Salt and freshly ground black
  pepper
Grated Parmesan cheese to
  serve

TORTELLINI WITH BROCCOLI, ANCHOVIES AND WALNUTS

SERVES
— 4 —

PREPARATION TIME
5 minutes
COOKING TIME
15 minutes

450 g (1 lb) fresh or *dried tortellini*
350 g (12 oz) broccoli florets
2 × 56-g (2-oz) cans anchovy fillets
2 tablespoons olive oil
50 g (2 oz) Parmesan cheese, finely grated
Salt and freshly ground black pepper
25 g (1 oz) walnuts, chopped

Tortellini are small, stuffed pasta circles and can be bought either dried or fresh. The dried variety is a handy store-cupboard stand-by and will keep almost indefinitely, while packs of fresh can be stored in the freezer until you need them and cooked straight from frozen. The sauce has a wonderful, strong flavour and although mixing meat and fish may seem odd, it goes well with tortellini stuffed with pork.

Cook the tortellini in plenty of boiling salted water until *al dente*; 10–12 minutes for dried pasta, 8–10 minutes for fresh. While the pasta is cooking, cook the broccoli in a separate pan of boiling salted water for 3–5 minutes until just tender.

Drain the oil from the anchovies into a pan, then chop the anchovies and add to the pan with the olive oil and cook for a minute or two. When the broccoli is ready, drain it and add to the anchovies. As soon as the pasta is cooked, drain at once in a colander. Tip the pasta into the pan with the anchovies, add the Parmesan cheese and plenty of freshly ground black pepper and scatter in the walnuts. Serve at once.

PASTA SPIRALS WITH MINCED PORK AND MUSHROOMS

S E R V E S

—— 4 ——

If you prefer, this sauce can be made hours in advance – or even the day before – and just re-heated while the pasta is cooking. Minced beef, lamb or even turkey could be used in place of the pork. The multi-coloured pasta looks delightful, but plain would be just fine as are other pasta shapes instead.

Heat the oil in a large pan and fry the shallots or onion and garlic over a medium heat until softened, but not brown. Stir in the pork and raise the heat. Cook, stirring, until the pork is well broken up and browned; about 5 minutes. Add the herbs, wine and seasoning and cook for a minute or two, then stir in the tomatoes and tomato purée. Cover and simmer for 20 minutes. Add the mushrooms and cook for about 10 minutes until the pork and mushrooms are tender and the sauce thickened.

While the sauce is cooking, cook the pasta spirals in plenty of boiling salted water until *al dente*; about 5 minutes for fresh, 10 minutes for dried. Drain in a colander and tip into the pork mixture. Using a wooden spoon toss the pasta to coat it with the sauce, then serve at once, with the basil or oregano leaves scattered on top.

INGREDIENTS

PREPARATION TIME
10 minutes
COOKING TIME
40 minutes

2 tablespoons olive oil
2 shallots or 1 small onion,
   peeled and finely chopped
1 garlic clove, peeled and
   crushed
450 g (1 lb) minced pork
1 tablespoon each chopped
   fresh basil and oregano or
   1 teaspoon each dried
150 ml (5 fl oz) dry white
   wine or light stock
Salt and freshly ground black
   pepper
425-g (15-oz) can chopped
   tomatoes
2 tablespoons tomato purée
175 g (6 oz) button
   mushrooms, quartered or
   halved if tiny
225 g (8 oz) fresh or dried
   pasta spirals (fusilli)
Few basil or oregano leaves
   to garnish

PASTA SHELLS WITH SPINACH, SMOKED HAM AND CHEESE

SERVES
— 4 —

PREPARATION TIME
10 minutes
COOKING TIME
20 minutes

350 g (12 oz) fresh or dried pasta shells
175 g (6 oz) frozen chopped spinach
100 g (4 oz) thick cut smoked ham, cubed
50 g (2 oz) Cheddar cheese, grated
2 tablespoons fresh breadcrumbs

FOR THE SAUCE
25 g (1 oz) butter
25 g (1 oz) plain flour
300 ml (10 fl oz) milk
50 g (2 oz) Cheddar cheese, grated
½ teaspoon Dijon mustard
Salt and freshly ground black pepper

With any luck, you'll have all the ingredients for this dish to hand – substitute crisp cooked bacon, or even left-over roast chicken or pork for the ham. Prepare it ahead of time, if you prefer, and either freeze for up to three months or chill for no more than a day or two. Thaw overnight in the fridge if frozen and re-heat in the oven at gas mark 5, 190°C (375°F) for about 30 minutes. If you want to freeze this recipe, remember to use an ovenproof dish that is freezer-proof too.

Cook the pasta shells in plenty of boiling salted water until *al dente*: about 10 minutes for dried, 3–4 minutes for fresh.

Meanwhile, put the spinach into a small pan with a little water and cook over medium heat until thawed, then continue cooking, stirring occasionally, until all the water has evaporated.

While the spinach is cooking, make the sauce. Melt the butter in a separate pan, stir in the flour and cook for 1 minute. Remove the pan from the heat and gradually stir in the milk. Return the pan to the heat and cook, stirring, until boiling and thickened. Stir in the cheese and mustard and add seasoning to taste.

As soon as the pasta is cooked, drain at once in a colander. Stir the pasta into the sauce with the ham and spinach and spoon into a buttered gratin dish. Mix together the cheese and breadcrumbs and sprinkle evenly over the top. Grill until the cheese is bubbling and golden. Serve hot.

MACARONI WITH CHICKEN, AUBERGINE AND OREGANO

S E R V E S
—— 4 ——

This is a delicious, if slightly unusual, sauce to serve with pasta. If you have a hearty appetite, add some chopped smoked bacon to the sauce with the chicken and serve with sautéed courgettes and some crunchy bread.

First make the sauce. Place the aubergine in a colander and sprinkle with salt. Leave to drain for 10 minutes, then rinse well and pat dry thoroughly on kitchen paper. Meanwhile, heat 2 tablespoons of the oil in a large frying-pan, add the onion and garlic and cook for 3 or 4 minutes to soften. Increase the heat, add the chicken and cook for 4–5 minutes until browned. Remove the chicken and onion mixture from the pan with a slotted spoon and set aside.

Add the rest of the oil to the pan and fry the aubergine over a high heat for 3–4 minutes until browned. Reserve a few olives for garnish and add the remainder to the pan along with the chicken and onion mixture, the tomatoes, tomato purée and half of the oregano. Season to taste and simmer gently while you cook the macaroni in plenty of boiling salted water until *al dente*, about 10–12 minutes. As soon as the macaroni is cooked, drain at once in a colander.

Tip the macaroni into the sauce and toss around with a wooden spoon until the macaroni is well coated. Serve at once with the reserved olives and the remaining oregano scattered on top.

INGREDIENTS

PREPARATION TIME
20 minutes
COOKING TIME
22 minutes

1 large aubergine, cut into 1-cm (½-in) cubes
4 tablespoons olive oil
1 onion, peeled and finely chopped
2 garlic cloves, peeled and crushed
350 g (12 oz) boneless chicken breasts, skinned and cut into 1-cm (½-in) cubes
10 stoned black olives, halved
425-g (15-oz) and 225-g (8-oz) can chopped tomatoes
2 tablespoons tomato purée
4 tablespoons oregano leaves, chopped
Salt and freshly ground black pepper
350 g (12 oz) macaroni

RAVIOLI WITH TOMATO AND PEPPER SAUCE

S E R V E S

— 3 —

PREPARATION TIME
5 minutes
COOKING TIME
25 minutes

350 g (12 oz) fresh ravioli
FOR THE SAUCE
2 tablespoons olive oil
*1 shallot or ½ small onion,
   peeled and finely chopped*
*1 garlic clove, peeled and
   crushed*
*1 yellow pepper, de-seeded,
   quartered and thinly sliced*
*6 tablespoons dry vermouth
   or white wine*
*425-g (15-oz) can chopped
   tomatoes*
2 tablespoons tomato purée
*4 tablespoons chopped fresh
   mixed herbs, such as
   parsley, thyme, basil and
   oregano*
*Salt and freshly ground black
   pepper*
*2 tablespoons chopped fresh
   mixed herbs to garnish*

In large supermarkets, look out for different flavoured canned tomatoes which will add an extra dimension to the sauce. Tomatoes with fennel are particularly good in this recipe, but those with added herbs would also be fine. Choose ravioli with a meaty filling, such as pork or beef, which goes well with the rich tomato sauce. The recipe can easily be stretched to serve four by increasing the ravioli to 450 g (1 lb). Serve with a bowl of crisp green salad and some warm ciabatta rolls.

Make the sauce first: heat the oil in a shallow pan and fry the shallot or onion with the garlic for 3–4 minutes until softened, but not brown. Stir in the pepper and cook for 2 or 3 minutes to soften, then stir in the vermouth or wine and allow to bubble for 1 minute before adding the tomatoes, tomato purée, herbs and seasoning. Bring to the boil, then reduce the heat and simmer, uncovered, for 10–15 minutes, stirring occasionally.

As soon as the sauce begins to simmer, heat the water for the ravioli, add salt and cook the ravioli until *al dente*; about 8–12 minutes. When it is cooked, drain at once in a colander. Tip the pasta out on to hot plates, spoon over the sauce and scatter with the herbs. Serve at once.

VEGETABLE LASAGNE WITH MOZZARELLA CHEESE

S E R V E S
— 6 —

Don't worry if you are missing a few of the vegetables in the recipe, you could also use mushrooms, aubergines, courgettes or peppers. Pre-cooked lasagne is easy to use because it can be layered with the sauces without boiling it first, but you need to make sure that the slices don't overlap. Cut them to fit your dish and make the lasagne in more layers if your dish is too small to take three sheets of lasagne along-side each other.

Pre-heat the oven to gas mark 6, 200°C (400°F).

Make the tomato sauce first: heat the oil in a pan and fry the onion over a low heat for about 5 minutes until softened. Add the garlic, carrots, celery and leeks and cook, stirring oc-casionally, for 5 minutes. Stir in the tomatoes and tomato purée, season to taste with salt and freshly ground black pep-per and simmer, uncovered, for 15 minutes.

While the tomato sauce is cooking, make the parsley sauce. Melt the butter in a pan, stir in the flour and cook for 1 minute. Remove the pan from the heat and gradually stir in the milk. Return the pan to the heat and cook, stirring, until boiling and thickened. Stir in the parsley and season to taste with salt and freshly ground black pepper.

Pour half of the tomato sauce into a large rectangular baking dish and arrange 3 sheets of lasagne on top. Add half of the cheese slices, pour over half of the parsley sauce and top with 3 more sheets of lasagne. Add the remaining tomato sauce, followed by the remaining lasagne, cheese and parsley sauce. Bake for 30–35 minutes, until the top is golden and bubbling. Serve hot with a dressed, crisp green salad.

INGREDIENTS

PREPARATION TIME
15 minutes
COOKING TIME
1 hour 15 minutes

9 sheets pre-cooked lasagne
225 g (8 oz) Mozzarella cheese, thinly sliced

FOR THE TOMATO SAUCE
2 tablespoons olive oil
1 onion, peeled and sliced
1 garlic clove, peeled and crushed
2 large carrots, diced
2 celery stalks, diced
2 leeks, sliced
425-g (15-oz) can chopped tomatoes
2 tablespoons tomato purée
Salt and freshly ground black pepper

FOR THE PARSLEY SAUCE
50 g (2 oz) butter
50 g (2 oz) plain flour
600 ml (1 pint) milk
3 tablespoons chopped fresh parsley
Salt and freshly ground black pepper

RAVIOLI WITH PINK PRAWN SAUCE

SERVES
—— 4 ——

Fresh ravioli is available, vacuum-packed, in super-markets. Choose a white fish or ricotta cheese and herb stuffing, if you have the choice, and go for green spinach pasta which makes a rather lovely colour contrast to the sauce. For the sauce fresh prawns are best but if you use frozen ones cook them straight from the freezer and, once heated through, lift out with a slotted spoon. Boil the sauce rapidly over a high heat to reduce before stirring in the cream and returning the prawns to the pan.

INGREDIENTS

PREPARATION TIME
5 minutes
COOKING TIME
15 minutes

350 g (12 oz) fresh ravioli
2 tablespoons olive oil
1 garlic clove, peeled and crushed
2 tablespoons tomato purée
Dash of hot pepper sauce
150 ml (5 fl oz) dry white wine
225 g (8 oz) shelled, cooked prawns
100 g (4 oz) mangetout, cut into pieces
300 ml (10 fl oz) single cream
A little freshly grated nutmeg
Salt and freshly ground black pepper
Few shredded basil leaves to garnish

Cook the ravioli in plenty of boiling salted water until *al dente*, about 8–12 minutes.

Meanwhile, heat the oil in a large pan and fry the garlic over a medium heat for a minute or two. Stir in the tomato purée, hot pepper sauce and the white wine and simmer for 3–4 minutes. Reduce the heat, add the prawns and mangetout and cook for 2 minutes. Stir in the cream, nutmeg and seasoning and heat through gently. Don't leave it simmering, if the pasta isn't ready, remove from the heat and re-heat only when needed.

As soon as the ravioli is cooked, drain at once in a colander. Tip the pasta into the sauce and toss gently to combine the two. Serve at once with the shredded basil scattered over the top.

PENNE WITH FOUR CHEESES

SERVES
—— 4 ——

These slim long tubes are cut diagonally so they actually scoop up the sauce as you eat, although other tubular pastas such as macaroni or rigatoni would do just as well. For the sauce, almost any hard cheese can be used, there's no need to stick to the ones I've suggested – it's a handy way to use up any odds and ends that you have in your fridge.

Cook the pasta in plenty of boiling salted water until *al dente*; dried pasta will usually take about 10 minutes, fresh between 2–4 minutes.

Meanwhile, make the sauce. In a large pan (so there's room enough for the pasta to be added later) melt the butter and stir in the flour. Cook over a low heat for about 1 minute, then remove from the heat and gradually stir in the milk. Return the pan to the heat and cook, still stirring, until the sauce is boiling and thickened. Stir in all but 4 tablespoons of the cheeses and season with salt and plenty of freshly ground black pepper.

As soon as the pasta is cooked drain at once in a colander and then add the pasta to the sauce. Stir well, then serve, sprinkled with the reserved cheeses and a little chopped fresh parsley or basil.

INGREDIENTS

PREPARATION TIME
5 minutes
COOKING TIME
15 minutes

350 g (12 oz) fresh or dried pasta quills (penne)
25 g (1 oz) butter
2 tablespoons plain flour
475 ml (16 fl oz) milk
75 g (3 oz) each Gouda, Mozzarella and Gruyère cheeses, coarsely grated
25 g (1 oz) Parmesan cheese, finely grated
Salt and freshly ground black pepper
Chopped fresh parsley or basil to garnish

BAKED TAGLIATELLE BOLOGNESE

S E R V E S
—— 4 ——

PREPARATION TIME
10 minutes
COOKING TIME
55 minutes

225-g (8-oz) fresh or dried
  tagliatelle
75 g (3 oz) Cheddar cheese,
  grated
2 tablespoons Parmesan
  cheese, finely grated
FOR THE SAUCE
2 tablespoons olive oil
1 small onion, peeled and
  finely chopped
1 carrot, finely chopped
1 celery stalk, finely chopped
100 g (4 oz) thick cut
  smoked bacon, diced
1 garlic clove, peeled and
  crushed
350 g (12 oz) minced lamb
150 ml (5 fl oz) dry white
  wine
225-g (8-oz) can chopped
  tomatoes
2 tablespoons tomato purée
Salt and freshly ground black
  pepper

Make the Bolognese sauce ahead of time, if you can. It will keep in the fridge for 1–2 days. Since the sauce also freezes extremely well, you could make two or even four times the recipe when you have the time and pack it in portions ready to use for this dish, or as a simple pasta sauce – just re-heat and serve over spaghetti – or use it to make a layered lasagne; follow the recipe for Vegetable lasagne with Mozzarella on page 93 and substitute this sauce for the tomato sauce.

———

Make the sauce first. Heat the oil in a large pan, add the onion, carrot and celery and cook over a medium heat until soft, but not browned. Raise the heat, add the bacon, garlic and lamb and cook until browned. Pour in the wine and cook until reduced by half. Add the tomatoes, tomato purée and seasoning, then cover and simmer for 40 minutes, stirring occasionally.

When the sauce is almost ready, cook the tagliatelle in plenty of boiling salted water until *al dente*; about 8 minutes for dried, 3–4 minutes for fresh. As soon as the tagliatelle is cooked, drain at once in a colander. Pour the sauce into a large, shallow ovenproof dish, tip the tagliatelle on top and spread out evenly. Scatter over the cheeses and grill until golden and bubbling. Serve at once.

RIGATONI SALAD WITH PEPPERS AND CAERPHILLY CHEESE

SERVES
—— 4 ——

This is a delicious mixture of flavours, the slight saltiness of the cheese just balanced by the sweet flavour of the peppers. I like to serve it warm rather than cold so the flavours really meld together. Choose ripe and fleshy peppers, red and yellow, or orange, ones are the best – don't use green peppers for this dish, they just don't have the right flavour. Rigatoni are fat, ridged tubes. You should be able to find them in a large supermarket, but if you can't, then substitute any other tubular pasta – or even pasta shells.

Cut the peppers into 4 or 5 pieces lengthways along the folds. Discard the seeds and core then, using a swivel action peeler, peel off the thin skin. Cut the peppers lengthways into fine strips, then cut the strips in half. Heat the oil in a large frying-pan and cook the peppers with the garlic, stirring occasionally, for about 5 minutes until softened.

Meanwhile, cook the rigatoni in a large pan of boiling salted water until *al dente*, about 10 minutes. As soon as the pasta is cooked, drain at once in a colander. Then tip the pasta into a bowl. Mix together the dressing ingredients, pour over the pasta and toss lightly to coat.

Add the peppers, basil and Caerphilly cheese and toss again. Serve warm with hot, buttered crusty bread.

INGREDIENTS

PREPARATION TIME
12 minutes
COOKING TIME
15 minutes

2 red and 2 yellow peppers
2 tablespoons olive oil
1 garlic clove, peeled and crushed
350 g (12 oz) rigatoni
25 g (1 oz) basil leaves
75 g (3 oz) Caerphilly cheese, roughly crumbled

FOR THE DRESSING
5 tablespoons olive oil
3 tablespoons white wine vinegar
Salt and freshly ground black pepper

TUNA, PASTA AND BROCCOLI BAKE

SERVES

— 4 —

PREPARATION TIME
10 minutes
COOKING TIME
50 minutes

225 g (8 oz) pasta spirals
(fusilli)
175 g (6 oz) broccoli, cut
into small florets
75 g (3 oz) Red Cheshire
cheese, crumbled
2 × 200-g (7-oz) cans
tuna fish in oil, drained
and roughly flaked
2 tablespoons fresh
wholemeal breadcrumbs
FOR THE SAUCE
50 g (2 oz) butter
50 g (2 oz) plain flour
600 ml (1 pint) milk
Salt and freshly ground black
pepper

The Red Cheshire cheese gives the sauce a lovely rosy glow. You could use Cheddar, either white or red (a mature one for flavour) or stick with the rosy glow and go for Red Leicester – both of these cheeses need to be grated coarsely as they won't crumble. Before the pasta goes into the oven, make sure that the broccoli is well covered with both the sauce and the breadcrumb topping or it may burn. Serve with sliced tomatoes in a herby dressing.

Pre-heat the oven to gas mark 4, 180°C (350°F).

Cook the pasta in plenty of boiling salted water until *al dente*, about 10 minutes. Cook the broccoli in a separate pan of boiling salted water for 2–3 minutes, until just tender. Drain.

While the pasta and broccoli are cooking make the sauce. Melt the butter in a large pan, stir in the flour and cook for 1 minute, then gradually stir in the milk and cook, stirring, until boiling and thickened. Remove the pan from the heat and stir in half of the cheese. Season to taste with salt and freshly ground black pepper.

As soon as the pasta is cooked, drain at once in a colander and then add to the sauce with the tuna and broccoli.

Tip the pasta mixture into a shallow ovenproof dish and spread evenly. Mix together the breadcrumbs and remaining cheese and scatter over the top. Bake for about 25 minutes until golden and crisp on top. Serve with sliced tomatoes in a herby dressing.

PASTA WITH CAULIFLOWER AND CHORIZO

SERVES
— 4 —

Delightful to look at as well as to eat, this pasta dish blends Spanish flavours with a touch of the Middle East. I know that cauliflower seems a strange partner for pasta, but if you cook the cauliflower until it is just crisp, and keep the pasta firm to the bite, then the two textures work really well together. If you can't find chorizo, use any other cooked, spicy sausages.

Cook the macaroni in a large pan of boiling salted water until *al dente*, about 10 minutes. While the pasta is cooking, cook the cauliflower in boiling salted water for 5 minutes, then drain.

Heat the oil in a large pan, add the garlic and chorizo sausages and fry for 2–3 minutes until golden. Then stir in the cauliflower, raisins and pine kernels and fry for 1–2 minutes until just beginning to colour. Season to taste with salt and freshly ground black pepper.

As soon as the pasta is cooked, drain at once in a colander and then tip into the cauliflower mixture and toss gently to mix. Serve at once with the grated Parmesan cheese handed separately.

INGREDIENTS

PREPARATION TIME
5 minutes
COOKING TIME
20 minutes

350 g (12 oz) macaroni
1 cauliflower, cut into tiny florets
4 tablespoons olive oil
2 garlic cloves, peeled and crushed
225 g (8 oz) chorizo sausages, thinly sliced
2 tablespoons raisins
2 tablespoons pine kernels
Salt and freshly ground black pepper
75 g (3 oz) Parmesan cheese, finely grated

PASTA BOWS WITH TROUT AND SUN-DRIED TOMATOES

SERVES
— 4 —

PREPARATION TIME
5 minutes
COOKING TIME
10 minutes

*350 g (12 oz) pasta bows
    (farfalle)*
50 g (2 oz) butter
350 g (12 oz) trout fillets
25 g (1 oz) plain flour
300 ml (10 fl oz) milk
1 teaspoon anchovy essence
1 egg yolk
2 tablespoons double cream
*75 g (3 oz) drained
    sun-dried tomatoes in
    olive oil, cut into thin
    strips*
*Salt and freshly ground black
    pepper*

Filleted trout is widely available in supermarkets now. It cooks very quickly and is ideal if you always find a whole trout just a little too much to eat. Sun-dried tomatoes, which have a wonderfully strong, sweet flavour are a delicious addition. The most widely available sun-dried tomatoes are those packed in jars of olive oil. If you happen to find the loose, dried ones you can use them too, just soak them in hot water to soften first. If you don't have a bottle of anchovy essence, then use Worcestershire sauce instead.

Cook the pasta in plenty of boiling salted water until *al dente*, about 10 minutes.

Meanwhile, cook the trout. Melt 25 g (1 oz) of the butter in a frying-pan and cook the trout for 5–6 minutes, turning once, until the flesh flakes easily. Lift the fish out of the pan, remove the skin and bones and break the fish into large flakes. Set the fish aside while you make the sauce. Melt the remaining butter in a large pan, stir in the flour and cook for 1 minute, then gradually stir in the milk and cook until boiling and thickened. Remove from the heat, beat together the anchovy essence, egg yolk and cream and beat into the sauce with the sun-dried tomatoes. Add the trout to the pan and fold in very gently.

As soon as the pasta is cooked, drain at once in a colander. Season to taste with salt and freshly ground black pepper, then arrange the pasta bows on hot plates and pour over the trout sauce. Serve at once.

R ICE

More rice is eaten worldwide than any other food, but in the past, in this country, we haven't made all that much use of it. We should though, since it is a truly amazing ingredient – it absorbs flavours, enhances others and even, as in the case of spicy hot foods, soothes and refreshes.

There was a time when long-grain was all that we could buy, but the range – even in supermarkets – has extended to include some wonderful varieties. Long-grain rice is the one we are most aware of, either plain white, or wholegrain or brown rice. Brown rice takes longer to cook but we should eat more of it as it has a lovely nutty texture and taste and is richer in minerals and vitamins than white rice.

Other rices are becoming increasingly available. Black, wild rice isn't really rice at all but a variety of grass used mainly (because it is expensive) as an addition to other rices. Risotto rice (arborio is the usual variety) is used almost exclusively for – you guessed it – risotto. Basmati rice is traditionally used for Indian dishes, but, since it has such a lovely fragrant flavour, I think it should be used more often in other recipes, or as a simple accompaniment.

Other grains, such as bulgar wheat, add a contrast of texture to rice dishes – try some of the new rice and grain combinations either as an accompaniment or in place of plain rice in recipes.

Since rice isn't a traditional British ingredient, many recipes in this chapter have their origins in other countries. You will be familiar with some, like Paella (see page 102), from holidays abroad. Other ideas have come from further afield, but are definitely worth tasting. Try them out – all I ask is that you don't (as the dinner ladies at my old school used to do) serve your rice dishes with chips!

PAELLA

S E R V E S
—— 6 ——

PREPARATION TIME
10 minutes
COOKING TIME
45 minutes

3 tablespoons olive oil
225 g (8 oz) boneless
   chicken thigh pieces,
   skinned and cut into large
   pieces
225 g (8 oz) chorizo or
   other spicy sausage,
   thickly sliced
1 large onion, peeled and
   chopped
1 red pepper, de-seeded and
   cut into short, thin strips
3 garlic cloves, peeled and
   crushed
350 g (12 oz) long-grain
   rice, washed and dried
1 tablespoon fresh thyme
   leaves
2 large pinches saffron
   threads
Salt and freshly ground black
   pepper
450 g (1 lb) mixed, cooked
   seafood

N ormally a bit of a fiddle to make, what with scrubbing
the mussels, peeling the prawns and sorting out the
squid. I've found that ready-prepared seafood – cooked squid
rings, prawns, mussels and cockles – is available in the chiller
cabinet of supermarkets and makes a wonderful substitute for
the real thing. Frozen prawns, canned mussels and cockles and
perhaps some canned tuna could be used instead.

Heat the oil in a large heavy-based sauté pan or a deep frying-
pan. Add the chicken and chorizo and fry over a high heat for
3–4 minutes until lightly browned. Stir in the onion, red
pepper and garlic and fry for 4–5 minutes until golden.
   Add the rice to the pan and stir until well coated in oil. Stir
in 1 litre (1¾ pints) water, the thyme and saffron, then season
to taste. Cover with a lid, bring up to the boil, then reduce the
heat and cook very gently for 20 minutes. Remove the lid,
add the seafood and stir gently. Cook over a low heat for 10
more minutes, stirring occasionally, until heated through.
Don't overcook the seafood, though, or it will begin to
toughen up. Serve at once.

Opposite: MEDITERRANEAN VEGETABLES STUFFED
WITH RICE AND NUTS (*page 113*)

SPICY CHICKEN PILAFF

SERVES

—— 4 ——

The blend of spices with more than a hint of cardamom gives this dish a lovely aromatic flavour but you could use 1–2 tablespoons of a ready-prepared spice mixture instead. Serve it hot, along with some cucumber raita; a mixture of thick yoghurt, finely diced cucumber and chopped fresh coriander or parsley, which you can make yourself in a minute or two. Or an easy alternative is a tub of ready-made tzatziki, the minty, Turkish or Greek yoghurt and cucumber mixture.

Heat the oil and butter together in a large, deep frying-pan and fry the onion and garlic over a medium heat for 5 minutes until softened. Add the peppers and cook, stirring, for 3 minutes. Raise the heat slightly, add the chicken strips and fry until golden brown. Stir in all the spices and cook for 1 minute, then add the rice and cook, still stirring, until well coated with butter, oil and spices. Add 750 ml (1 ¼ pints) of the stock and bring to the boil.

Reduce the heat, cover the pan and simmer for 15 minutes. Then stir in the peas and cook for about 5 minutes more until the rice is tender, but not too soft, and all the liquid is absorbed (add the remaining stock if necessary). Season to taste with salt and freshly ground black pepper and serve at once.

INGREDIENTS

PREPARATION TIME
10 minutes
COOKING TIME
35 minutes

2 tablespoons sunflower oil
25 g (1 oz) butter
1 onion, peeled and finely chopped
1 garlic clove, peeled and crushed
1 red and 1 yellow pepper, de-seeded and cut into strips
450 g (1 lb) boneless chicken breasts, skinned and cut into strips
1 teaspoon cardamom seeds, crushed or ground cardamom
½ teaspoon ground cinnamon
2 teaspoons ground cumin
1 teaspoon ground coriander
1 teaspoon ground turmeric
¼ teaspoon cayenne pepper
225 g (8 oz) long-grain rice
900 ml (1 ½ pints) hot chicken stock
100 g (4 oz) frozen peas
Salt and freshly ground black pepper

Opposite: WARM LENTILS WITH SMOKED BACON AND ROCKET (*page 119*)

MONKFISH AND PRAWN RISOTTO

SERVES

— 4 —

Arborio rice from Piedmont in northern Italy is becoming increasingly available in supermarkets, where it is sometimes labelled simply as risotto rice. The grains are slightly plump and of medium length and when cooked absorb a great deal of liquid without becoming too soft – so the finished risotto is creamy, but the grains still have a slight bite. Serve with a mixed green salad.

Heat the oil in a large shallow pan and fry the onion and garlic for 3–5 minutes until soft, but not browned. Stir in the rice until well coated with oil, then add a ladleful of fish stock and allow the liquid to become absorbed before adding the next. Stir constantly over a medium heat, while you continue to add stock and cook the rice.

After about 10 minutes, when the rice should be about half cooked, add the prawns and monkfish to the pan and stir them into the rice. Pour in the wine and cook for 3–4 minutes, before adding more stock. Season to taste and continue cooking and adding stock until the rice is tender, but still firm to the bite, and the monkfish is cooked. Stir in the parsley and serve hot.

INGREDIENTS

PREPARATION TIME
15 minutes
COOKING TIME
30 minutes

4 tablespoons sunflower oil
1 large onion, peeled and finely chopped
2 garlic cloves, peeled and crushed
225 g (8 oz) arborio risotto rice
About 1.25 litres (2 ¼ pints) hot fish stock
150 g (5 oz) cooked, peeled prawns
225 g (8 oz) monkfish, cut into 2.5-cm (1-in) cubes
150 ml (5 fl oz) dry white wine
Salt and freshly ground black pepper
2 tablespoons chopped fresh parsley to garnish

LEEK AND GRUYÈRE RISOTTO TART

SERVES

—— 6 ——

Not a tart in the sense that we know it with a pastry base, this is just risotto baked in a flan tin. So if you are in a real hurry, you could omit the eggs and serve it straightaway. However, when the risotto is baked the outside becomes lovely and crisp and makes a wonderful contrast to the soft, cheesy rice inside. It is delicious served hot, but is equally good warm, or cold.

Melt the butter in a heavy-based frying-pan and fry the onion and garlic for 3–5 minutes until softened. Stir in the rice until well coated in butter, then pour in the wine and cook until the wine has been absorbed. Add a ladleful of stock and cook until absorbed, then continue cooking for about 20 minutes, adding the stock a ladleful at a time, until all the liquid is absorbed and the rice is tender.

Meanwhile, heat the oil in a large pan and cook the leeks over a medium heat for about 10 minutes, stirring occasionally, until softened and just beginning to brown.

Pre-heat the oven to gas mark 6, 200°C (400°F). Grease and base-line a deep 23-cm (9-in) loose-bottomed flan tin (or use a deep, spring-clip tin).

Mix the leeks into the rice, then add the eggs, 50 g (2 oz) of the Gruyère cheese, the crème fraîche or soured cream, parsley and nutmeg, then season to taste with salt and freshly ground black pepper and mix well. Spoon the risotto into the tin and spread evenly. Sprinkle over the remaining cheese and bake for 25 minutes until the tart is golden and set. Serve warm or cold. Cut into wedges with a dollop of extra crème fraîche or soured cream.

INGREDIENTS

PREPARATION TIME
10 minutes
COOKING TIME
50 minutes

50 g (2 oz) butter
1 onion, peeled and finely chopped
1 garlic clove, peeled and crushed
225 g (8 oz) arborio risotto rice
150 ml (5 fl oz) dry white wine
450 ml (15 fl oz) hot vegetable stock
2 tablespoons olive oil
450 g (1 lb) leeks, thinly sliced
2 eggs, beaten
60 g (2½ oz) Gruyère cheese, finely grated
50 g (2 oz) crème fraîche or soured cream plus extra for serving
3 tablespoons chopped fresh parsley
Large pinch of grated nutmeg
Salt and freshly ground black pepper

SPICY KEDGEREE

S E R V E S
—— 4 ——

This traditional breakfast dish, a mixture of flavoured rice, smoked haddock and chopped boiled eggs, makes a wonderful supper! Buy the smoked haddock fillets (uncoloured if you can) fresh, vacuum-packed or frozen.

Place the haddock fillets in a large, shallow pan, add 1 litre (1 ¾ pints) water, the stems from the parsley (reserve the leaves for garnish), lemon slices and peppercorns. Bring to the boil, then reduce the heat and simmer gently for about 10 minutes until the fish is tender. Lift out the fish with a slotted spoon and leave to cool. Strain the cooking liquid and reserve 900 ml (1 ½ pints).

While the fish is cooking, melt 25 g (1 oz) of the butter in a pan over a low heat and fry the onion for 3–5 minutes to soften. Stir in the rice and spices and cook for 1–2 minutes, pour in the reserved cooking liquid and season to taste. Bring to the boil, then reduce the heat and simmer, stirring occasionally, for 20–25 minutes until the rice is tender and the liquid absorbed.

While the rice is cooking, boil the eggs for 8 minutes, then shell and cut into large chunks. Remove the skin and bones from the fish and break the flesh into flakes. When the rice is cooked, stir in the fish and eggs, along with the remaining butter, cut into pieces. Serve hot, sprinkled with the reserved parsley leaves. Delicious!

INGREDIENTS

PREPARATION TIME
5 minutes
COOKING TIME
30 minutes

750 g (1 ½ lb) smoked haddock fillets
A few sprigs of flat leaf parsley
½ lemon, sliced
A few peppercorns
50 g (2 oz) butter
1 small onion, peeled and finely chopped
225 g (8 oz) long-grain rice
½ teaspoon ground cumin
½ teaspoon ground cardamom
Salt and freshly ground black pepper
3 eggs

CHICKEN BIRYANI

S E R V E S
—— 4 ——

Basmati rice is a slender long-grain rice grown in the foothills of the Himalayas. Its name means 'fragrant' and true to this, once cooked, it has a lovely, distinctive aroma and taste. You could use long-grain rice instead, but the finished dish won't taste quite the same. If you don't have any whole spices, use ground cardamom and cumin instead – and if you have neither then, at a push, you could use a tablespoon or two of curry powder in place of all the spices.

Heat 4 tablespoons of the oil in a large heavy-based pan, add the cardamom pods, cumin seeds and turmeric and fry for 1 minute. Stir in the onions, garlic and ginger and cook over a medium heat for 5 minutes until softened. Lift the onion mixture out of the pan with a slotted spoon and set aside.

Add the chicken to the pan, raise the heat and fry the chicken for about 5 minutes until browned all over. Stir in the rice and cook for 2–3 minutes. Stir in the yoghurt a tablespoon at a time, then pour in the stock and add the seasoning. Cover the pan and simmer for 25–30 minutes until the rice and chicken are tender.

When the biriani is nearly ready, heat the remaining oil in a small pan and fry the almonds, sultanas and chillies for a minute or two until the almonds are golden. Serve the biriani hot with the almond mixture and coriander or parsley leaves scattered over the top.

INGREDIENTS

PREPARATION TIME
15 minutes
COOKING TIME
1 hour

5 tablespoons sunflower oil
6 green cardamom pods, bruised
1 teaspoon cumin seeds
½ teaspoon ground turmeric
2 onions, peeled and finely sliced
2 garlic cloves, peeled and crushed
5-cm (2-in) piece fresh root ginger, peeled and grated
550g (1 ¼ lb) chicken breasts, skinned and cut into thin strips
450g (1 lb) basmati rice, washed thoroughly
150 ml (5 fl oz) natural yoghurt
750 ml (1 ¼ pints) hot chicken stock
Salt and freshly ground black pepper
25g (1 oz) flaked almonds
25g (1 oz) sultanas
1–2 red chillies, de-seeded and finely sliced
3 tablespoons shredded coriander or flat leaf parsley leaves to garnish

FRUITY RICE SALAD WITH GRILLED CHICKEN

S E R V E S

— 4 —

INGREDIENTS

PREPARATION TIME
10 minutes
COOKING TIME
20 minutes

3 tablespoons sunflower oil
1 small onion or 2 shallots,
  finely chopped
225 g (8 oz) long-grain rice
600 ml (1 pint) hot chicken
  stock
4 boneless chicken breasts,
  about 175 g (6 oz) each
Salt and freshly ground black
  pepper
1 orange
1 canned pimento, diced or
  50 g (2 oz) mixed sliced
  peppers in oil, drained
1 avocado, peeled, stoned
  and diced
6 stoned black olives, halved

FOR THE DRESSING
5 tablespoons sunflower oil
2 tablespoons white wine
  vinegar
¼ teaspoon Dijon or
  wholegrain mustard
Salt and freshly ground black
  pepper
1 tablespoon each chopped
  fresh parsley and mint

In the summer-time you could barbecue the chicken outside to serve with the rice salad, which, if you prefer, can be left to cool once it is mixed. Swap the orange for a fresh mango, or some canned mango in natural juice, for a change. Canned mango needs only to be drained and chopped. If you use a fresh mango, cut it into three flat thick slices (the stone will be in the centre section), then cut the flesh from the outside pieces into cubes and cut the flesh away from the stone.

Heat 2 tablespoons of the oil in a large pan and fry the onion or shallots over a medium heat for 3–5 minutes, stirring occasionally, until softened.

Add the rice and stir until well coated in oil. Pour in the hot stock and bring to the boil. Reduce the heat, cover the pan, and cook for about 20 minutes until the rice is tender and the stock absorbed.

Meanwhile, slash the chicken breasts two or three times through the skin with a large sharp knife and brush them with the remaining oil. Season well with salt and freshly ground black pepper and grill for about 8 minutes, turning occasionally, until the outsides are browned and the inside cooked through, but still moist.

While the chicken and rice are cooking, make the dressing by mixing together the oil, vinegar, mustard with salt and freshly ground black pepper to taste, then stir in the parsley and mint. Remove all the peel and white pith from the orange with a serrated knife, then cut the segments away from the membrane; work over a bowl as you do this to catch the juice. Tip the rice into the bowl with the orange juice and stir in the dressing, pimento or peppers, avocado and olives. Mix well and serve at once with the chicken.

NUTTY RICE AND BULGAR SALAD

S E R V E S

—— 4 ——

This is one of those extremely versatile recipes, which you can vary according to what's in the cupboard. Use all rice, or all bulgar wheat, or a ready-made mixture of rice, grains and spices if you want. Just make the total weight the same. Use a large pinch or two of cayenne or chilli powder if you have no fresh chillies. You could also use up any little pieces of red, yellow or green peppers that you have in the fridge, by slicing them and adding to the pan with the rice.

Place the bulgar wheat in a bowl with 450 ml (15 fl oz) boiling water and leave to soak for 15 minutes; fluff up with a fork occasionally. Cook the rice in boiling salted water for 10–12 minutes until tender. Meanwhile, make the dressing, mix together the vinegar and oils with plenty of salt and freshly ground black pepper, then set aside.

Heat the 2 tablespoons of olive oil in a small frying-pan and fry the hazelnuts, pine kernels, raisins and chillies for 2–3 minutes over a medium to high heat, stirring occasionally, until browned.

Drain the rice, rinse in cold water, then drain again thoroughly. Place in a large bowl with the bulgar wheat, add the apricots, meat and herbs and mix well. Stir in the dressing, then spoon over the hot nut and raisin mixture and serve at once.

INGREDIENTS

PREPARATION TIME
5 minutes
COOKING TIME
20 minutes

225 g (8 oz) bulgar wheat
175 g (6 oz) long-grain rice
2 tablespoons olive oil
100 g (4 oz) hazelnuts,
  roughly chopped
4 tablespoons pine kernels
25 g (1 oz) raisins
1–2 fresh red chillies,
  de-seeded and finely sliced
100 g (4 oz) ready-to-eat
  dried apricots, sliced
100 g (4 oz) cooked lamb,
  ham or beef, sliced and
  cut into strips
6 tablespoons mixed chopped
  fresh parsley, thyme and
  mint

FOR THE DRESSING
4 tablespoons white wine
  vinegar
6 tablespoons olive oil
4 tablespoons hazelnut or
  sunflower oil
Salt and freshly ground black
  pepper

BROWN AND WILD RICE SALAD WITH TUNA, PEPPERS AND MUSHROOMS

SERVES

—— 4 ——

PREPARATION TIME
10 minutes
COOKING TIME
18 minutes

*225 g (8 oz) mixed brown
long-grain rice and wild
rice*
2 eggs
*100 g (4 oz) tiny button
mushrooms, halved*
*2 spring onions, sliced
diagonally*
*1 red and 1 yellow pepper,
de-seeded, quartered, and
thinly sliced*
*225-g (8-oz) can tuna fish
in oil, drained*
*50 g (2 oz) stoned black
olives, halved*
FOR THE DRESSING
*2 tablespoons white wine
vinegar*
6 tablespoons olive oil
½ teaspoon Dijon mustard
*Salt and freshly ground black
pepper*
*3 tablespoons chopped fresh
parsley*

There are all sorts of rice mixtures available in super-markets and specialist grocers, some have spices and herbs added, which make a welcome addition to this dish. If you have no time to shop, vary the salad according to what you have already in the cupboard and freezer – plain long-grain or brown rice; some frozen peas, green or broad beans, boiled until tender; a few chopped sun-dried tomatoes or a drained can of pimento, shredded. All of them make quite good substitutes if you are short of one or two fresh ingredients.

Cook the rice mixture in a pan of boiling salted water for 15–18 minutes or until tender and then drain.

Meanwhile, hard-boil the eggs for 8 minutes, then cool under cold running water. Make the dressing by mixing together the vinegar, oil, mustard and salt and freshly ground black pepper – do this either by shaking the ingredients together in a screw-topped jar, or by whisking them in a small bowl. Set aside.

As soon as the rice is cooked, transfer it to a large bowl. Add the parsley to the dressing and give it another mix, then pour over the hot rice and stir well. Mix in the mushrooms and leave it all to cool a little while you shell the eggs and cut them into small wedges. Mix the eggs into the rice with the spring onions, peppers, tuna and olives and serve still warm with crusty bread or a leafy green salad.

MEDITERRANEAN VEGETABLES STUFFED WITH RICE AND NUTS

SERVES
——— 4 ———

Variations of these flavoursome, filled vegetables are made in myriad ways all over the Mediterranean. Peppers and large flat field mushrooms can be stuffed in the same way. In the Middle East, where this dish is called Kizi-inzi, which means 'one for you and one for me', a huge dish of different vegetables are made, then placed in the middle of the table and each person chooses a different one in turn.

Prepare the vegetables: cut the aubergines and courgettes in half lengthways and scoop out the centres using a spoon (leave the shells about 5 mm, ¼ in, thick). Chop the flesh into small pieces and set aside. Cut the tomatoes in half around their equators and scoop out the flesh and seeds into a bowl, then leave them upside down on kitchen paper to drain, while you make the stuffing.

Heat the oil in a pan and fry the onion and garlic, stirring occasionally, for 5 minutes until softened and beginning to brown. Add the chopped aubergine and courgette flesh with the tomato pulp and fry for 3–5 minutes until softened. Stir in the rice, cinnamon or allspice and the cayenne pepper. Cook, stirring, for 1–2 minutes, then pour in the stock and bring to the boil. Reduce the heat, cover the pan and simmer for 10–15 minutes until the rice is tender and all the liquid has been absorbed. Pre-heat the oven to gas mark 6, 200°C (400°F).

While the stuffing is cooking, bring a large pan of water to the boil and blanch the aubergine and courgette shells for 2 minutes. Drain, then rinse them with cold water and leave to drain upside-down on kitchen paper.

When the rice is cooked, remove the pan from the heat and stir in the parsley, lemon juice, almonds and pumpkin seeds and season to taste with salt and pepper. Pile the stuffing into the vegetable shells and arrange, close together, in one or two greased baking dishes. Pour 4 tablespoons of water into each dish and bake for 20 minutes until the vegetable shells are just tender. Serve hot or warm.

INGREDIENTS

PREPARATION TIME
20 minutes
COOKING TIME
50 minutes

2 medium aubergines
2 large courgettes
2 beefsteak tomatoes
1 tablespoon olive oil

FOR THE STUFFING
2 tablespoons olive oil
1 onion, peeled and chopped
1 garlic clove, peeled and crushed
175 g (6 oz) long-grain rice
½ teaspoon ground cinnamon or allspice
½ teaspoon cayenne pepper
450 ml (15 fl oz) vegetable or chicken stock
2 tablespoons chopped fresh parsley
1 tablespoon lemon juice
50 g (2 oz) blanched almonds, chopped
2 tablespoons pumpkin seeds
Salt and freshly ground black pepper

JAMBALAYA

S E R V E S

—— 4 ——

The real thing, as it is cooked in the southern states of America, would have whole mussels, clams and prawns as well as the odd crab claw or shelled lobster stirred into the rice. However, a mixture of ready-prepared seafood, such as prawns, squid rings and mussels, makes a surprisingly creditable – and much easier – alternative. Serve hot with garlic bread.

Heat the oil in a large pan and fry the bacon until crisp. Lift out of the pan with a slotted spoon and drain on kitchen paper. Add the onion, celery and rice to the pan and cook, stirring, for 3–4 minutes. Stir in the chilli powder, then add three-quarters of the stock and the bay leaf. Cover the pan and simmer for 10 minutes. Add the green pepper and the tomatoes and simmer for 5 minutes, then stir in the seafood, chicken and cooked bacon. Cook for about 5 minutes until heated through, stirring in a little more of the stock, if necessary, to keep it moist. Season to taste with salt and freshly ground black pepper, then scatter over the parsley and serve hot.

INGREDIENTS

PREPARATION TIME
12 minutes
COOKING TIME
30 minutes

1 tablespoon olive oil
*4 back bacon rashers,
  chopped*
1 onion, peeled and chopped
3 celery stalks, sliced
225 g (8 oz) long-grain rice
¼ teaspoon chilli powder
*450 ml (15 fl oz) hot
  chicken shock*
1 bay leaf
*1 large green pepper,
  de-seeded and chopped*
*425-g (15-oz) can chopped
  tomatoes*
*450 g (1 lb) cooked mixed
  seafood, such as mussels,
  prawns and squid*
*100 g (4 oz) cooked chicken
  breast, diced*
*Salt and freshly ground black
  pepper*
*1 tablespoon chopped fresh
  parsley*

MUSHROOM RISOTTO

S E R V E S

—— 4 ——

A selection of mushrooms is best for this dish, choose a mixture of shiitake, chestnut and oyster mushrooms to add colour and plenty of flavour. Button mushrooms are fine, but it is worth adding a few soaked, dried mushrooms for flavour – small sachets of dried porcini mushrooms can be found in Italian delis and some large supermarkets, or use dried shiitake mushrooms which are sold loose, and at a very reasonable price, in Chinese supermarkets. Dried mushrooms need to be soaked in warm water to reconstitute them before using; so do this before you start.

———

Heat the butter and oil in a heavy-based pan and fry the onion and garlic over a medium heat for about 5 minutes until softened and beginning to brown. Add the mushrooms and cook for 2–3 minutes. Stir in the rice until well coated in oil and butter, then pour in a ladleful of the stock and, stirring occasionally, simmer gently until the liquid is absorbed.

Add more stock a ladleful at a time and continue cooking, stirring occasionally, until all the liquid is absorbed and the rice is just cooked. Add salt and freshly ground black pepper to taste, then serve hot, with the parsley and Parmesan cheese scattered on top.

INGREDIENTS

PREPARATION TIME
5 minutes
COOKING TIME
30 minutes

40 g (1 ½ oz) unsalted butter
1 tablespoon olive oil
1 small onion, peeled and finely chopped
1 garlic clove, peeled and crushed
350 g (12 oz) mushrooms, sliced
350 g (12 oz) arborio risotto rice
About 1 litre (1 ¾ pints) hot chicken or vegetable stock
Salt and freshly ground black pepper
TO SERVE
2 tablespoons chopped fresh parsley
50 g (2 oz) Parmesan cheese, pared into thin shavings

FAST FRIED RICE

S E R V E S

—— 4 ——

This dish is great for using up left-overs, I've added prawns, but cooked chicken, beef or fish – even a can of tuna or salmon – can be added instead. Add a crushed garlic clove with the ginger, if you like, and splash in a little light soy sauce just before you serve the rice.

INGREDIENTS

PREPARATION TIME
10 minutes
COOKING TIME
20 minutes

225 g (8 oz) long-grain rice
100 g (4 oz) frozen peas
2 tablespoons stir-fry, chilli or sunflower oil
2.5-cm (1-in) piece fresh root ginger, peeled and finely grated
1 small onion, peeled and finely chopped
75 g (3 oz) button mushrooms, sliced
3 eggs, beaten
200-g (7-oz) can sweetcorn, drained
175 g (6 oz) cooked, peeled prawns
Salt and freshly ground black pepper

Cook the rice in a large pan of boiling salted water for 10–12 minutes until tender. Meanwhile, cook the peas in boiling salted water for 2–3 minutes until just tender, then drain.

Heat the oil in a large frying-pan or wok, add the ginger and onion and stir-fry for 2–3 minutes. Add the mushrooms and stir-fry for 2 minutes.

When the rice is cooked, drain thoroughly and add to the pan. Cook over a high heat for 3 minutes, then stir in the eggs and cook, stirring, for 1 minute. Add the peas, sweetcorn and prawns and cook for 2 minutes until heated through. Season to taste with salt and freshly ground black pepper and serve at once.

LENTILS AND BEANS

I love lentils – I was literally brought up on lentil soup. The huge pot boiling away on the stove, with a ham shank and lots of root vegetables for flavour, is one of my strongest childhood memories.

Like rice and grains, lentils absorb other flavours and are extremely versatile. They can be cooked to a purée, or prepared more quickly so they hold their shape and texture. Yet, along with beans, they have a rather worthy reputation and are often considered both brown and boring. As you will discover, they can be used to prepare dishes that are neither of these.

Lentils, although they are dried, cook remarkably quickly, and don't need to be soaked first. The smallest red ones cook in only 15 minutes, and even the largest green lentils are soft in about 30 minutes. Dried beans, though, aren't much use for quick meals, since they require overnight soaking and long boiling to soften them, but canned beans are a different story and there are at least ten varieties easily available in large supermarkets.

Lentils and beans make lovely vegetarian dishes to serve in their own right, yet they also go well with meat and can be turned into substantial, hearty fare. What is less well known is that they don't have to be hearty. Combined with cheese, fish or vegetables, lentils and beans can be turned into lovely light meals too – as you will see.

RED LENTIL
AND
CARROT BURGERS

SERVES
—— 4 ——

PREPARATION TIME
25 minutes
COOKING TIME
30 minutes

225 g (8 oz) red lentils
1 large carrot, diced
350 ml (12 fl oz) vegetable
stock
1 tablespoon sunflower oil
1 onion, peeled and finely
chopped
1 teaspoon ground cumin
1 teaspoon ground coriander
¼ teaspoon chilli powder
Salt and freshly ground black
pepper
100 g (4 oz) porridge oats
1 egg, beaten
Sunflower oil for frying

If you have the ingredients to hand, you'll have time to whizz up some tomato sauce to serve with these vegetarian burgers while they are cooking (see page 62, omitting the bacon), although a dollop of tangy chutney or – dare I say it! – tomato ketchup will do just as well. Use breadcrumbs to coat the burgers if you have no porridge oats. Serve with a salad.

Place the lentils and carrot in a pan with the stock and bring to the boil. Partially cover the pan and simmer gently for 15–20 minutes until the lentils and carrot are just tender and the stock absorbed.

Meanwhile, heat the oil in a pan and cook the onion for 5 minutes until softened. Stir in the cumin, coriander and chilli powder and cook for 3 minutes. When the lentils and carrot are cooked tip them into the pan with the onion, spices and salt and pepper to taste. Mix well and leave to cool.

When the mixture is cool, shape into 8 flat round cakes. Put the porridge oats on a plate and the beaten egg on another, then dip the burgers first in egg, then in oats to coat completely.

Heat the oil in a large frying-pan and fry the burgers for 6–8 minutes, turning once, until brown and crisp. Drain on kitchen paper and serve hot.

WARM LENTILS WITH SMOKED BACON AND ROCKET

SERVES
— 2 —

Canned green lentils make for a much speedier salad, but they have less of a bite than freshly cooked ones, which in any case need no soaking and take only 20 minutes to cook. Rocket or roquette is a fairly fashionable salad leaf – it looks somewhat like dandelion leaves and has a wonderfully strong, nippy flavour. Supermarkets for some reason sell rocket in tiny packets which make it rather expensive to serve as a salad in its own right, so use baby spinach leaves instead, if you prefer – or even some very finely shredded savoy cabbage.

Wash the lentils in a sieve under cold running water, then cook them, with the bay leaf, in boiling salted water for about 20 minutes until just tender.

Meanwhile make the dressing: mix together the shallot, garlic, vinegar, both oils and salt and freshly ground black pepper to taste, either by shaking them in a screw-topped jar or whisking in a small bowl.

About 5 minutes before the lentils are ready, melt the butter in a frying-pan and fry the bacon for 4–5 minutes until cooked and browned. Drain the lentils, remove the bay leaf, then pour over the dressing and toss lightly.

Arrange the rocket on serving plates, spoon the warm lentils on top, scatter over the parsley and serve at once with the bacon, either left in whole rashers or cut into thin shreds – whichever you prefer.

INGREDIENTS

PREPARATION TIME
5 minutes
COOKING TIME
30 minutes

225 g (8 oz) green lentils
1 bay leaf
25 g (1 oz) butter
8 thick, smoked back bacon
  rashers, de-rinded
50 g (2 oz) rocket
2 tablespoons chopped fresh
  parsley

FOR THE DRESSING
1 shallot, peeled and finely
  chopped
½ garlic clove, peeled and
  crushed
2 tablespoons white wine
  vinegar
3 tablespoons olive oil
2 tablespoons walnut oil
Salt and freshly ground black
  pepper

LENTIL AND RICE SALAD

SERVES

—— 4 ——

PREPARATION TIME
30 minutes
COOKING TIME
20 minutes

225 g (8 oz) green lentils
100 g (4 oz) long-grain rice
1 carrot, coarsely grated
4 spring onions, finely sliced
1 teaspoon caraway seeds
50 g (2 oz) unsalted
    peanuts, toasted
2 tablespoons each chopped
    fresh thyme and parsley
4 tablespoons mayonnaise
4 tablespoons strained Greek
    yoghurt
A dash of hot pepper sauce
1 tablespoon lemon juice
Salt and freshly ground black
    pepper
225 g (8 oz) tomatoes,
    thinly sliced

If you want to make this look a little more special, you can pack the salad into a savarin ring mould. Place a large serving plate on top of the mould then, holding both firmly together, quickly invert, give them a sharp shake – just once should be enough – and carefully lift off the mould. Arrange the tomato slices around the edge before you serve.

Wash the lentils, then cook in salted boiling water for about 20 minutes until just tender. Meanwhile, cook the rice in boiling salted water for 10–12 minutes until just tender, then drain the lentils and rice and tip them together into a large bowl. Stir in the carrot, spring onions, caraway seeds, peanuts and half the thyme and parsley and toss lightly together.

In a small bowl, mix together the mayonnaise, yoghurt, hot pepper sauce and lemon juice with salt and freshly ground black pepper to taste and stir roughly into the salad. Arrange the tomato slices in a circle on a serving plate and spoon the lentil salad into the middle. Scatter the remaining thyme and parsley over the top and serve at once.

TEXAS CHILLI

SERVES

—— 4–6 ——

This is a very expandable recipe. If you've lots of friends arriving for a cheap and cheerful supper, add one or even two more cans of kidney beans and make up the sauce with one more can of chopped tomatoes. I'm almost afraid to specify the quantity of chilli powder that you need, so much depends on the hotness of your particular brand – and, of course, how hot you like your chilli.

Heat the oil in a large heavy-based pan and cook the onion, garlic and green pepper for about 5 minutes until softened. Add the chilli powder or chillies and hot pepper sauce, if using, and fry for 1 minute. Add the minced beef, turn up the heat and cook for 5 minutes more, stirring occasionally, until the mince is well broken up and browned.

Stir in the tomatoes, tomato purée and oregano, then season to taste with salt and freshly ground black pepper. Bring the chilli to the boil, then reduce the heat, cover and simmer for 30 minutes, stirring occasionally. Stir in the beans and simmer for 10 minutes more. Serve hot.

INGREDIENTS

PREPARATION TIME
5 minutes
COOKING TIME
50 minutes

2 tablespoons olive oil
1 onion, peeled and chopped
2 garlic cloves, peeled and
  crushed
1 green pepper, de-seeded
  and chopped
1–2 tablespoons chilli powder
  or 2 fresh green chillies,
  de-seeded and chopped
A dash of hot pepper sauce
  (optional)
450g (1 lb) minced beef
2 × 425-g (15-oz) cans
  chopped tomatoes
2 tablespoons tomato purée
2 tablespoons chopped fresh
  oregano or 1 tablespoon
  dried
Salt and freshly ground black
  pepper
2 × 425-g (15-oz) cans
  red kidney beans, drained
  and rinsed

GRILLED PORK CHOPS WITH SAUCY GREEN BEANS

SERVES
— 4 —

In the summer-time use fresh broad beans instead of frozen and you might like to add a little chopped fresh sage for extra flavour. Later on, towards autumn, if the skins of the broad beans are a little tough, then pop them out of the skins, by squeezing each between your fingers, to reveal the bright green bean inside; it's a bit of a fiddle, but if you enlist some help it will only take a few minutes. This is fairly filling but, if you are really hungry, mashed potatoes are good to serve on the side to mop up the sauce.

Brush a little oil over the chops, sprinkle them with salt and freshly ground black pepper and grill, brushing them occasionally with oil, for about 8 minutes, until just cooked and browned on both sides. Don't overcook the chops – pork can become very dry.

Meanwhile, cook the French and broad beans in separate pans of boiling salted water for 3–5 minutes until just tender – the French beans should still be quite crisp.

While the beans are cooking, make the sauce. Melt the butter in a small pan and stir in the flour. Cook for 1 minute, then remove the pan from the heat and gradually add the milk. Return the pan to the heat and cook, stirring constantly, until the sauce boils and thickens. Stir in the flageolet beans, mustard and salt and freshly ground black pepper to taste and simmer gently on a low heat. As soon as the beans are ready, drain them and stir them into the sauce. Add the cream and serve at once with the chops.

INGREDIENTS

PREPARATION TIME
10 minutes
COOKING TIME
20 minutes

1–2 tablespoons olive oil
4 pork chops, about 175 g (6 oz) each
Salt and freshly ground black pepper
100 g (4 oz) fine French beans, halved
175 g (6 oz) broad beans
425-g (15-oz) can flageolet beans, drained and rinsed

FOR THE SAUCE
25 g (1 oz) butter
25 g (1 oz) plain flour
450 ml (15 fl oz) milk
1 teaspoon wholegrain mustard
Salt and freshly ground black pepper
2 tablespoons double cream

BUTTER BEANS AND LAMB WITH A CRUMBLY CRUST

SERVES
— 4 —

We are more used to having a crumble on puddings, yet they make a good savoury topping and are much easier and quicker to do than a pastry crust. Use a well-flavoured cheese such as a mature Cheddar. Pumpkin and sesame seeds add a nice nuttiness to the crumble, but you can omit them if you have none or add sunflower seeds or chopped nuts, such as hazelnuts, almonds, peanuts or cashews, instead. Serve hot with braised leeks or cabbage.

Pre-heat the oven to gas mark 5, 190°C (375°F).

Heat the oil in a large pan and fry the chops over a high heat for 3–5 minutes until browned on both sides. Remove the chops with a slotted spoon and set aside. Add the onion and garlic to the pan and cook for 5 minutes until softened. Add the carrots and cook for 2–3 minutes more, then sprinkle over the flour and cook, stirring, for a minute or two. Pour in the lamb stock and bring to the boil, stirring until thickened. Return the lamb chops and any juices to the pan, then cover, reduce the heat and simmer for 15 minutes, stirring occasionally.

While the lamb is cooking, make the crumble topping. Sift the flour into a bowl with a little salt and rub in the butter until the mixture resembles breadcrumbs. Stir in the grated cheese and the pumpkin and sesame seeds, then season to taste with salt and freshly ground black pepper.

When the lamb has finished cooking, stir in the butter beans, parsley and mint and season to taste with salt and freshly ground black pepper. Spoon the chops and bean mixture into a greased ovenproof dish, then sprinkle the crumble mixture on top and bake for 30 minutes until the crumble is crisp and golden brown. Serve hot.

INGREDIENTS

PREPARATION TIME
10 minutes
COOKING TIME
1 hour 5 minutes

2 tablespoons olive oil
4 leg of lamb chops or chump chops
1 onion, peeled and finely chopped
1 garlic clove, peeled and crushed
2 carrots, thickly sliced
2 tablespoons plain flour
300 ml (10 fl oz) lamb stock
425-g (15-oz) can butter beans, drained and rinsed
1 tablespoon each chopped fresh parsley and mint
Salt and freshly ground black pepper

FOR THE CRUMBLE TOPPING
225 g (8 oz) plain flour
100 g (4 oz) butter
3 tablespoons grated Cheddar cheese
2 tablespoons pumpkin seeds
1 tablespoon sesame seeds

SAUSAGE, BACON AND BEAN CASSOULET

SERVES

—— 4 ——

Fairly cheap and cheerful, yet very tasty. You could get away with using plain old bangers, but a mix of herby and spicy sausages (such as chorizo or kabanos) does give the cassoulet a lovely flavour.

———

Pre-heat the oven to gas mark 4, 180°C (350°F).

Heat the oil in a large, flameproof casserole, add the bacon, onions and garlic and fry for 5–6 minutes until the onions have softened and the bacon is lightly browned. Add the sausages and fry for 5 minutes. Stir in the tomatoes, tomato purée and stock, then add the bay leaf and thyme and bring to the boil. Stir in the beans and season to taste with salt and freshly ground black pepper.

Cover the casserole, transfer to the oven and cook for 30 minutes. Remove the casserole from the oven, sprinkle over the breadcrumbs and bake, uncovered, for a further 15 minutes until the breadcrumbs are golden brown. Serve immediately.

INGREDIENTS

PREPARATION TIME
20 minutes
COOKING TIME
1 hour

2 tablespoons olive oil
225 g (8 oz) smoked bacon
  chops, diced
2 onions, peeled and
  chopped
2 garlic cloves, peeled and
  crushed
225 g (8 oz) smoked spicy
  sausages, thickly sliced
225 g (8 oz) small herby
  sausages, halved
425-g (15-oz) can chopped
  tomatoes
2 tablespoons tomato purée
150 ml (5 fl oz) beef stock
1 bay leaf
A few sprigs of fresh thyme
400-g (14-oz) can haricot
  or black-eyed beans,
  drained and rinsed
Salt and freshly ground black
  pepper
100 g (4 oz) fresh
  breadcrumbs

Mediterranean haricot bean salad

S E R V E S

—— 4 ——

I f, like me, you never know what you are going to eat tomorrow, beans from a can are almost as good as dried ones (though usually a little softer) so long as you rinse them thoroughly to get rid of the brine.

Place the beans, tuna, feta cheese, tomatoes, cucumber and olives in a large bowl and toss together lightly. Make the dressing: mix together the vinegar, oil and salt and freshly ground black pepper to taste, either by shaking them in a screw-topped jar or whisking in a small bowl. Pour the dressing over the salad and mix gently. Using a pair of scissors, snip thin shreds of basil over the salad and serve with slices of floury ciabatta bread to mop up the dressing.

INGREDIENTS

PREPARATION TIME
20 minutes
COOKING TIME
none

2 × 425-g (15-oz) cans
haricot beans, drained and
rinsed
225-g (8-oz) can tuna fish
in oil, drained
100 g (4 oz) feta cheese,
diced
225 g (8 oz) small tomatoes,
halved (or cut into thin
wedges, if too large)
10-cm (4-in) piece cucumber,
diced
50 g (2 oz) stoned black
olives, shredded
Small handful basil leaves

FOR THE DRESSING
4 tablespoons balsamic or
white wine vinegar
7 tablespoons olive oil
Salt and freshly ground black
pepper

RAGOUT OF BROAD BEANS, POTATOES AND LEEKS

SERVES

—— 4 ——

Vegetarians will enjoy this just as it is. If you are a confirmed meat eater then grill lamb or bacon chops to serve with the ragout, which will then serve six. If you don't have double cream in the fridge, then reduce the stock to 300 ml (10 fl oz) and add 200 ml (7 fl oz) milk along with the stock. You can miss out the cumin too, if you prefer, or add a tablespoon or two of wholegrain mustard or ready-made pesto instead.

———

Heat the oil in a large, shallow pan and cook the leeks over a medium heat for 3 minutes until softened. Add the potatoes, raise the heat slightly, and cook for about 5 minutes until just beginning to brown. Stir in the flour and cumin and cook for 1 minute. Pour in the stock and cook, stirring constantly, until boiling and thickened. Season to taste with salt and freshly ground black pepper, then reduce the heat, cover the pan and simmer for 15 minutes.

Stir in the broad beans and cook, stirring occasionally, for 5 minutes until the leeks and potatoes are tender. Add the cream and snipped chives and simmer for a minute or two, then serve hot with bread to mop up the sauce.

INGREDIENTS

PREPARATION TIME
10 minutes
COOKING TIME
40 minutes

2 tablespoons olive oil
4 leeks, sliced
450 g (1 lb) new potatoes, scrubbed and diced
2 tablespoons plain flour
1 teaspoon ground cumin
450 ml (15 fl oz) vegetable stock
Salt and freshly ground black pepper
350 g (12 oz) frozen broad beans
4 tablespoons double cream
4 tablespoons snipped fresh chives

BUTTER BEAN AND CHESHIRE CHEESE FLAN

SERVES
—— 4 ——

Cheshire cheese has a lovely, light, slightly salty taste. I've chosen Red Cheshire for its colour in this recipe, but use the others if you prefer – or substitute a good mature Cheddar instead. Cheshire is a crumbly cheese so break it up with your fingers rather than grating. Leave it in largish pieces about the size of hazelnuts and they will transform into little melting nuggets in the finished dish. Serve with a salad.

Pre-heat the oven to gas mark 6, 200°C (400°F).

Roll out the pastry and use it to line a 20-cm (8-in) flan tin, trim the edges neatly, then prick the base lightly and chill for 10 minutes. Line the pastry case with greaseproof paper, fill with baking beans (dried butter beans are ideal for this task, but any dried bean or even rice will do) and bake for 10 minutes.

Meanwhile, prepare the filling. Place the spinach in a small pan with 2 tablespoons of water and cook over a low heat until thawed and quite dry. Beat together the eggs, cream or milk and nutmeg, salt and freshly ground black pepper to taste (remember the Cheshire cheese is quite salty), then stir in the spinach.

Remove the pastry case from the oven and lift out the paper and baking beans. Spoon the butter beans into the pastry case and spread evenly. Scatter over the Cheshire cheese, then carefully pour over the egg mixture. Reduce the oven temperature to gas mark 4, 180°C (350°F) and bake for about 30 minutes until the egg mixture is just set and the top golden brown. Serve hot or just warm.

INGREDIENTS

PREPARATION TIME
20 minutes
COOKING TIME
40 minutes

175 g (6 oz) ready-made wholemeal or shortcrust pastry

FOR THE FILLING
50 g (2 oz) frozen chopped spinach
2 eggs, beaten
150 ml (5 fl oz) single cream or milk
A little freshly grated nutmeg
Salt and freshly ground black pepper
425-g (15-oz) can butter beans, drained
100 g (4 oz) Red Cheshire cheese, roughly crumbled

CARROT, BROCCOLI AND LENTIL QUICHE

S E R V E S

—— 4 ——

INGREDIENTS

PREPARATION TIME
10 minutes
COOKING TIME
1 hour 10 minutes

175 g (6 oz) ready-made wholemeal or *shortcrust pastry*

FOR THE FILLING

50 g (2 oz) brown lentils, washed

100 g (4 oz) carrots, sliced

100 g (4 oz) broccoli, cut into tiny florets

2 eggs, beaten

200 ml (7 fl oz) single cream or *milk*

Salt and freshly ground black pepper

2 tablespoons chopped fresh parsley

75 g (3 oz) Wensleydale cheese, coarsely grated

Wensleydale cheese is one of Yorkshire's best-kept secrets. It is traditionally eaten with fruit (they have a saying, that an apple pie without the cheese is like a kiss without the squeeze!) and its subtle flavour is delicious too with the sweet taste of carrots. Lancashire cheese also goes well with both sweet and savoury foods and could be used instead.

Pre-heat the oven to gas mark 6, 200°C (400°F).

Cook the lentils in boiling salted water for 30 minutes until just tender. Meanwhile, roll out the pastry and use it to line a 20-cm (8-in) flan tin. Trim the edges neatly, then prick the base lightly and chill for 10 minutes. Line the pastry case with greaseproof paper, fill with baking beans (dried butter beans are ideal for this task, but any dried bean or even rice will do) and bake for 10 minutes.

Meanwhile, prepare the filling: cook the carrots and broccoli in separate pans of boiling salted water until just tender. Beat together the eggs, cream or milk, season with salt and freshly ground black pepper to taste and stir in the parsley. Drain the lentils, carrots and broccoli as soon as they are cooked, rinse in cold water to cool a little and drain again.

Remove the pastry case from the oven and lift out the paper and baking beans. Spoon the lentils, carrots and broccoli into the pastry case and spread evenly. Scatter over the Wensleydale cheese, then carefully pour over the egg mixture. Bake for about 30 minutes until the egg mixture is just set and the top golden brown. Serve hot or just warm.

CHICK PEA MOUSSAKA

S E R V E S
— 4 —

This vegetarian version of the traditional Greek dish works extremely well – you'd hardly notice that the meat was missing. It is a bit of a fiddle, as there are two sauces plus the aubergines to cook. However, if you can manage to cook more than one thing at a time – or get some help – it is not too tricky and it is in the oven for half of the cooking time.

Pre-heat the oven to gas mark 5, 190°C (375°F).

Arrange the aubergine slices in a colander, sprinkling them with salt as you go. Leave them to drain for 10 minutes, then rinse them thoroughly and pat dry very well on kitchen paper.

While the aubergines are draining, heat 2 tablespoons of the oil in a pan and fry the onion and garlic for 5 minutes, or until softened. Stir in the cinnamon, mushrooms and courgettes and cook for 2–3 minutes more. Add the tomatoes, tomato purée, basil or parsley and salt and freshly ground black pepper to taste and bring to the boil. Simmer, uncovered, for 10 minutes, then stir in the chick peas.

Heat 2 tablespoons of the oil in a large frying-pan and fry the dried aubergine slices over a high heat until golden brown on both sides. Cook in batches and add extra oil, if necessary. Drain the aubergine slices on kitchen paper.

While the aubergines are cooking, make the topping. Melt the butter in a small pan and stir in the flour. Cook for 1 minute, then remove the pan from the heat and gradually stir in the milk. Return the pan to the heat and cook, stirring, until boiling and thickened. Remove from the heat again and beat in the cheese and egg. Season to taste with salt and freshly ground black pepper.

Grease an ovenproof dish and arrange one third of the aubergines in the base. Add half of the tomato and chick pea mixture, then one third of the aubergines, the remaining tomato and chick pea mixture and, finally, the remaining aubergines. Pour the cheese sauce over the top and spread to cover evenly. Bake for 40–45 minutes until the topping is softly set and golden brown. Serve at once.

INGREDIENTS

PREPARATION TIME
15 minutes
COOKING TIME
1 hour 5 minutes

2 aubergines, sliced
4–6 tablespoons olive oil
1 onion, peeled and chopped
1 garlic clove, peeled and
   crushed
½ teaspoon ground cinnamon
75 g (3 oz) button
   mushrooms, sliced
175 g (6 oz) courgettes,
   sliced
425-g (15-oz) can chopped
   tomatoes
2 tablespoons tomato purée
1 tablespoon chopped fresh
   basil or parsley
Salt and freshly ground black
   pepper
425-g (15-oz) can chick
   peas, drained and rinsed

FOR THE TOPPING
25 g (1 oz) butter
25 g (1 oz) plain flour
300 ml (10 fl oz) milk
100 g (4 oz) Cheddar
   cheese, grated
1 egg, beaten
Salt and freshly ground black
   pepper

VEGETARIAN COTTAGE PIE

SERVES

—— 4 ——

INGREDIENTS

PREPARATION TIME
15 minutes
COOKING TIME
1 hour

100 g (4 oz) brown lentils, washed
1 kg (2 lb) potatoes, peeled
50 g (2 oz) bulgar wheat
425 ml (15 fl oz) boiling vegetable stock
2 tablespoons olive oil
2 onions, peeled and finely chopped
8 ready-to-eat stoned prunes, chopped
50 g (2 oz) blanched almonds, chopped
2 teaspoons yeast extract
Salt and freshly ground black pepper
25 g (1 oz) butter
3 tablespoons milk

'What! Prunes in cottage pie,' I hear you say, 'how odd.' Yet prunes (which many of us view with suspicion, in remembrance of school dinners) have been used in savoury dishes for centuries. The French use them in all sorts of recipes. In this dish I think you will find that they are surprisingly good. Use the semi-dried variety, which don't need to be soaked. Serve the pie with carrots and peas – ordinary ones, or mangetout.

———

Cook the lentils in boiling salted water for about 30 minutes, until tender. Meanwhile, cook the potatoes in boiling salted water for 20 minutes until tender and soak the bulgar wheat in the boiling stock for 10–15 minutes.

Pre-heat the oven to gas mark 5, 190°C (375°F).

When the lentils are almost ready, heat the oil in a large pan and fry the onions for 5 minutes until softened, then stir in the lentils, bulgar wheat and stock, prunes, almonds and yeast extract. Season to taste with salt and freshly ground black pepper and leave to simmer for 5 minutes.

Drain the potatoes as soon as they are cooked and mash while still warm with the butter, milk and plenty of freshly ground black pepper. Spoon the lentil mixture into a shallow baking dish, spread the mashed potato evenly on top and mark roughly with a fork. Bake for about 30 minutes until the potato is golden brown. Serve at once.

INDEX

Page numbers in *italic* refer to colour photographs

131